THE KINDNESS CURRICULUM

HOW TO SUPPORT YOUR CHILD'S
LEARNING AND EMOTIONAL WELLBEING

GEOFF BIDDALL

ISBN: 9798268633733

Printed in 2025 by Amazon KDP

All names and identifying details have been changed to protect the privacy of children, families, and colleagues. Any resemblance to real persons is coincidental.

The information in this book is provided for educational and wellbeing purposes. It is not intended as professional medical or psychological advice. Readers should always seek the guidance of qualified professionals regarding any concerns.

To Scarlett, Connie and Immy, the kindest people I know.
And to Dad, you always taught me to "go for it", so here goes.

CONTENTS

PART III

The "Extras" – Special Educational Needs,
being "More Able", Homework and screen time

INTRODUCTION

The first time I stood in a Primary School classroom since being a pupil in the 90s was when I began work experience. I had decided that I wanted to change career and do something I had always planned to do, I just didn't know when. What an experience it was.

The tables felt tiny, like I was a character in a pedagogical Alice In Wonderland. Brightly coloured displays filled almost every inch of wall space, packed with diagrams, examples of children's learning, the latest maths topic (multiplying 4-digit by 2-digit numbers), timetables of the week, children's birthdays and the map of where to stand in the event of a fire alarm. The tiny tables were oriented toward a vast digital "smartboard"; quite the step up from the overhead projectors I used to see in class which shone a light through a sheet of printed plastic to cast the image on a blank board. The smartboard displayed a lesson starter activity on it, and the teacher could move elements around or write directly on it with a stylus. Imagine a PowerPoint presentation built for children, as that is exactly what it is.

In the centre was Mr Elliott, part CBeebies presenter, part motivational speaker, part lecturer – and completely captivating. I was 30 years old then and I was probably more engaged and hooked than the children were!

The lesson aim was to be able to "show not tell" how a character was feeling. Mr Elliott was showing the children a selection of freeze frames from animated films and the children had to explain what they thought the character was feeling and give evidence for why they thought this. Whilst the children were generating ideas, Mr Elliott was simultaneously ensuring engagement by asking children for their thoughts, handing out examples on paper and noticing and correcting poor behaviour or lack of focus. I felt the entire lesson was a resounding success and after one hour all children seemed to have made progress and enjoyed discussing their thoughts and ideas. I could not believe that Mr Elliott could maintain this level of connection and engagement for 5 more hours that day, but he absolutely did.

Every day that I had free I would come back in to the school and spend time in a different class. Every time I was amazed to see that, whilst delivery was different depending on the teacher and specific lesson, the quality of the teaching seemed to be flawless.

As I started my Post Graduate Certificate of Education I was assigned to a class with Miss Leach. Over time, I would take the lead on more and more lessons until my course was finished and I was expected and able to take the lead of the class for the whole day.

Soon it was my job to guide the 32 children of "Class 5B" through all of the joy, hardships, singing, arguing and learning of a typical day in a UK Primary school. What an honour it was to be given that level of responsibility for our children and to be energised and exhausted in equal measure each day.

I describe my experiences as a teacher developing from complete novice to staff member to illustrate just how *excellent* I believe that quality of education to be in the UK. When you leave your child at the classroom door in the morning, or wave them off on the bus, you can be confident that they will have every opportunity to learn, experience new things and develop their understanding of every-thing the National Curriculum states that children have to learn in this country.

However, this book wouldn't be much use to you or I if it just con-tained the gushing praise of a teacher about his colleagues.

Whilst my confidence in teachers and schools to deliver high qual-ity learning is more or less unshakeable, I feel we as a community are overlooking the greatest source of growth for our children: a focus on supporting their emotional wellbeing. It is my firm belief and my lived experience that by orienting ourselves towards un-derstanding children's internal struggles, validating them and guid-ing them towards understanding themselves better, we can help to raise happier and more mentally healthy children. As a result, and as a positive consequence rather than a primary aim, I believe their academic achievement will necessarily improve and we will all reap the benefits of our children moving closer toward their potential.

This book distils six years of classroom teaching and private tuition of children from the ages of 6 to 16. I do not claim to be the most organised or effective teacher to grace the profession, far from it. But one thing I can say proudly is that I know the children in my care better than most. It might seem to go beyond the remit of what we expect from teachers today but I aim to teach the children in my classes like my own kids. To expect the best from them. To assume good intentions. To have patience in their difficult moments and to listen to what they have to say, not to act like I care, but because I truly do.

In order to share what I have found to be the most effective strategies to support children in school, I have separated this book in to three main parts:

Part 1 – The Kindness Curriculum: Subjects

Part 2 – Subject specific support to help you as a parent understand what to focus on to help your child's learning.

Part 3 – The "Extras" – These include Special Educational Needs, "More Able" provision, Homework and how to support your child at home.

This book will make most sense when read in that order, but of course you are welcome to focus on whichever section is most pressing or of most interest to you, and they are written, in the main, as standalone elements.

WHY I WROTE THIS BOOK

Teachers are a naturally chatty group, but from the hundreds of parents I have spoken to over the years there seems to remain a mystique around what their children do in the classroom and how they can be best supported.

Young people grow and develop so quickly that as soon as we feel we understand one stage of their life, it has changed and there are new topics to learn and pressures to handle. Through after-school conversations or phone calls made after a minor incident in school, I have noticed that almost all parents wanted to share more about their children and wanted a better insight on what I was doing and why. The more I shared, the better I could collaborate with parents and it felt like a team effort in raising and educating their children in the optimal way for everyone. Simply put, once parents could see I wanted the same things for their child that they did, everything improved.

I wrote this book to remove the mystery around what happens in the classroom, to reassure parents that the school is on their side and to give practical guidance around what I have seen to work best.

This isn't a book packed with empirical studies and quotes, that is by design. I have learned what helps children to be happier, less anxious and achieve more, through hundreds of days of classroom experience. I believe that knowledge is something we should all have access to.

THE EDUCATIONAL LANDSCAPE IN THE UK

Before beginning, I think it is useful for me to explain the current state of the UK school system. As with this guide in general, this will be mostly focused around primary schools rather than secondary, but I believe this will be useful for a parent of a child of any age.

The Department for Education (DfE) is the UK Government organisation that is responsible for education and wider skills across England. It sets budgets and priorities for all education establishments. This matters to you as a parent, and me as a teacher because the DfE priorities filter down through school management and result in tangible changes to the education offering. The basic flow is as follows:

DfE priorities set

School management adapt

Teachers and teaching adapt

The children adapt.

Even in 2025, the attainment priorities are reading, writing and maths. Therefore, as schools know they will be judged to be effective if their students achieve well in these three areas then school management orient their teaching and learning strategy to focus on these subjects, teachers prioritise these subjects and children spend the majority of their time improving their skills and knowledge in these areas.

Why does this matter to you, as a parent? Simply put, it affects what your child will be learning each day and what metric they will be measured against to judge their "success" academically.

At primary level, children are not scrambling to achieve qualifications for their later life and as such, parents could theoretically ignore these measures with no real impact to you or your child. But you and I both know that your child's attainment, or struggles therein, *do* have a tangible effect on their view of themselves so it is not an easy position to take.

Further, as children progress through primary school, they begin to become more aware of where they find themselves in "pecking order" within the classroom in reading, writing and maths.

In one of my Year 6 classes, I had a boy who I shall call Tony. You can guess that I've changed his name as you don't find too many "Tony"'s in primary school these days. I've changed the name of every student I make reference to but each story does relate to a real person in one of my classes; using vague theories or imagined scenarios would not provide the authenticity needed to make this book useful to you.

Tony seemed generally disinterested in school, not disruptive for the sake of it, but more distracted and he struggled to keep up with the complexity of the learning in class. Tony had the support of a

Teaching Assistant (TA) for most lessons and this didn't ever seem to faze him. However, one day as the school year progressed, I commented to Tony about how well he was doing in his maths learning. His response: "I'm terrible at it. That's why I always need Mrs H (the TA) with me." As his teacher, all I could see was how much better he could calculate and how much quicker he was at his times tables, but for Tony, he was constantly judging himself in comparison to others based on how much teacher support he was getting.

I don't believe Tony had, or has, any aspirations to go in to a career that makes use of maths knowledge. But children are incredibly insightful when it comes to their own assessment of their place within a group and the fact that schools prioritise maths as a key part of the curriculum meant that Tony judged himself to be a failure. As a teacher, nothing saddens me more than to see a child develop this kind of negative self-image. Thankfully, that isn't the end of Tony's story and I will speak more about him later.

As the saying goes, 'what gets measured gets managed.' The danger is, schools end up measuring test scores more than feelings and children start believing those scores define them.

I can appreciate the value of Key Performance Indicators (KPIs) as a means to remain objective about what is working and what isn't; we have to be very careful about which metrics we decide to focus on. KPIs don't exist for our feelings, so we decide that we will measure scores instead. It is my firm belief that if we shift our focus away from scores and test results and do everything in our power to support our children's emotional development then we will find ourselves with a much healthier, happier AND more productive and successful generation of young people.

PART I

THE KINDNESS CURRICULUM

When I began my Postgraduate Certificate in Education (PGCE – the teaching qualification in the UK) in 2017, my life was hectic. I had decided to leave the Police and do something I loved, and that was empowering and daunting in equal measure. On top of that, my wife was in the middle of her first pregnancy and my father was in intensive care with double pneumonia and a host of other health complaints. As we rushed to visit him one night, me wearing a now slightly ragged shirt and tie from a day shadowing teachers in school and my wife sporting a rather large baby bump, I was pretty convinced he wouldn't make it to see the birth of our daughter. I was silently crying behind my wife, watching dad touch her baby bump and try desperately to maintain a smile for her. He was sat up in a hospital bed, his face completely encased in a clear plastic ventilator mask which was meant to assist his breathing and to clear fluid from his lungs. Everything felt like it was falling apart and I wondered if I had made the right choice.

Every day was busy, I was operating on very little sleep and my thoughts were consumed by worry about dad and my wife and whether they were ok. Thankfully, dad recovered to a more stable state but the concerns about his health continued for many months to come. During the PGCE course, I was either in University attending lectures on teaching theory, or I was in a classroom trying to put that theory in to practice in short teaching sessions, designed for me to gradually build up my teaching time and move towards leading my own class. My teaching mentor was Miss Leach; an amazingly capable, caring and talented educator. The lecturers at the University were engaging and helpful. However, when it came to learning what I needed to, my head was simply elsewhere. Despite my absolute passion for the course and future ahead of me, that amount of worry and fear floating around in my head was overwhelming. The quality of the guidance I was receiving at the time could not have been better. But here's what I realised; If your emotional needs aren't met, the quality of teaching makes almost no impact at all.

My circumstances were difficult for a time, but I know that every person reading this will be able to remember a time of similar emotional tension. Maybe you're in that place right now. If you are, I commend you for even thinking of reading a book that helps you to support the people around you. That takes a lot of strength.

All of us know pain of some kind and, on reflection, we all know that when we are emotionally frazzled we can become impatient, withdrawn, bad tempered, distracted, tearful or even dissociate completely. Now consider our children. They feel all those emotions, likely at a greater intensity and without the life experience we all have to talk ourselves down and think, "I know this will be alright in the end." Adding academic pressure on top of that is a recipe for disaster and the best teaching in the world will make very little difference at all.

The Kindness Curriculum consists of guidance to support your children through difficulties that they will all naturally surface, at differing times and in varying amounts: Anxiety, Friendship Issues, Failure, Confidence and Resilience. Unlike traditional subjects at school, there are no specific terms and times when these lessons should be taught. They are relevant to all children at some point in their school life. Anxiety might seem to be a topic that doesn't need discussing, right before an event hits your lives that causes it to become a necessary focus. Conversely, low confidence might have always been a feature of your family, but that may well recede as you use the guidance in this book and apply it at home.

It is my hope that the subjects of The Kindness Curriculum become taught in school and at home as comprehensively as maths and english taught today. As we will see, an understanding of the difficulties of being a young person in school and having support with these unavoidable facts of life can and will have a hugely positive impact on children's learning and development as a whole.

It is not intended to replace the curriculum in the education system where you live. The aim of The Kindness Curriculum is to enhance our children's experience of school and unlock their full potential as people first and learners second.

ANXIETY

Anxiety is part of the normal spectrum of emotions and a feeling, albeit an uncomfortable one, that we all know. Many of us might even admit that it is the driving force behind a lot of our productivity. The fear of "falling behind" or not being enough appears to be a powerful motivator for people to work extremely hard and push themselves. Rarely do I see an ambitious adult who seems serene and driven purely by their desire to meet their potential. Much more often I can detect a frantic undercurrent of "I really must get this done!"

Anxiety, in this form, seems to push us from behind as if we've just stepped on an escalator before we're ready, frantically buttoning up our work shirts whilst simultaneously trying to regain our balance. For many of us, it's all we've ever known and as such we might not even label our actions as an anxious or fear-based response. To be clear, anxiety can aid us in getting an awful lot of work done and in our age of "hustle and grind", this scattered productivity can be looked upon favourably by our managers, co-workers and anyone trying to get ahead.

As parents of school-age children, you would be forgiven for thinking that a level of anxiety is baked-in to the process of getting children to school. I have had countless debates about how certain socks "feel wrong" on my daughters' feet, how the breakfast options that were satisfactory yesterday are now suddenly outrageous and about how we manage to be almost late to school each day regardless of the time we start our day. The time slips away and everyone gets more and more rushed until we reach the crescendo of the classroom door when peace can once again return.

As a teacher, the end of the getting ready process transitions in to the beginning of a full school day. Entering a brightly lit and brightly coloured classroom filled with 30 other children without any time to decompress before learning begins must be challenging for even the most serene and emotionally resilient children.

If we as adults struggle to name anxiety, imagine how hard it is for your child. What you will hear are complaints about stomach aches, feeling hot, a worry about something seemingly unimportant "I'm just worried I don't know my 7 times tables!" or anything in between. Our tendency can be to try and fix that particular ailment and move our child on through their day, but that is missing the point. What underlies these ostensibly odd complaints is a worry about something a little deeper and we need to take time to tease that out before we can cool off and release that feeling.

A classroom example

In one of my Year 6 classes, I had a brilliant student who I will call Oriana. Oriana had a supportive family, a lovely friendship group and she always contributed well in lessons.

I had first noticed her a year before she joined my class. I would often see her sat at a table in the main atrium, outside her classroom looking tearful and glazed. On speaking with her teacher at the time, Oriana would frequently complain of stomach aches and seem to have an inability to focus on any learning on some days. There didn't seem to be a clear reason for this and there was no known health problem. At times I would speak to her and ask if she was OK, trying to build a little rapport, knowing that there was a chance she would be in my class in the next academic year. In our school there were two Year 5 classes and you wouldn't know until the end of the academic year which class you would be inheriting.

I was pleased when Oriana and her group joined my class and it became apparent quite quickly that the stomach aches she was experiencing seemed to be very much linked to times when she felt pushed out of her friendship group or in some way confused about her place within it.

My strategy to help Oriana wasn't particularly technical, I just wanted to get to know her better and dig in to the trigger points of what was making her upset. I have found that naming the issue as I see it can offer a child an opportunity to honestly admit the root cause of the problem. The conversation went something like this:

"Oriana, I'm not you so I can't be sure whether you really do have stomach pain, it just seems to me that when you and Emily (her best friend) aren't getting on, it seems to really affect you and I'm wondering if you're actually feeling worried instead of poorly?"

"I really don't feel well, my stomach does actually hurt."

"I know, but do you feel like these fallouts sometimes make you feel worse? Like a buzzy, worried feeling that you feel in your stomach?"

"It is a bit like that, yeah."

In follow-up conversations, I would be more direct and ask if anything had happened with her friends. Quite quickly, Oriana was able to see the link between friendship worries and physical feelings. As she was a very reflective person for her age, we both began to realise that her friendship with Emily had been fracturing for a while and they had remained "best friends" more out of routine than a genuine shared connection. I asked Oriana if there was anyone outside her friendship group that she liked in the class. She said she had always liked Jess but hadn't really spoken to her much as she was always with Emily.

During the next classroom seat move, I crafted it so that Oriana and Jess sat together, a long way away from Emily. Over time, Oriana's real personality began to grow and watching her become more confident and happy was a true joy to see. She was smiling more and contributing more often in lessons. My teaching remained the same but Oriana flourished and her SATs scores were some of the best I've ever seen.

No scheme of learning could ever hope to generate the improvements in the quality of learning that I saw and I am certain that helping to fix her friendship issues reduced her anxiety and enabled her to reach her potential in Year 6.

Fundamentally, knowing your child or even endeavouring to find out more about what scares them can be transformative. It is never really about the stomach aches or not knowing what a subordinating conjunction is (I'm still not sure I know what a subordinating conjunction is without checking the lesson plan first). Ask your children about their learning. Not what score they got on the test but how the test made them feel. Do they feel pressure to perform or compete with others? Open the dialogue and let the clues behind the anxiety pour out. Only then can you begin to tactfully unpick their concerns and you might just find they begin to fix their problems for themselves, with your support.

Key lessons:

- Anxiety is a normal human emotion that everyone feels.

- Anxiety could hold back your child's progress at school more than any difficulty with learning.

- Talk and value any issue they face. Feeling heard and understood could be transformative.

FRIENDSHIPS

As we have seen in the case of Oriana, even a healthy friendship can restrict a child and hold them back from being their best. As a teacher, friendship issues take up more non-learning time and generate more parent-teacher meetings than any other issue, and it isn't even a close contest.

A classroom is a fantastic place for learning: each child has support materials, teaching assistants and visual aids at their fingertips at a moment's notice. Interactive whiteboards, craft materials and new research provide interesting sources of information on a huge range of topics. However, we should not overlook that the classroom is a living group of young people who are at all times interacting with each other. The "vibe" of a class is almost tangible at times and it is my job as a teacher to manage and guide that feel towards the learning, diffuse issues when I see them and know when to demand focus and when to back off to allow breaks in play.

Sometimes though, no amount of enthusiasm or even a break to watch an animated video about the learning is enough to break a child out of the smothering feeling that something is wrong in their friendship group.

I'd wager that you hear more about friendships than you do about actual learning from your child. Ask what the topic was in maths and the stock answer is "I don't remember." But ask how everyone else is at school and you're far more likely to get a download about how Person A and Person B seemed to be leaving your child out, looking at them in a strange way in the classroom or having a dispute at playtime. It is our natural tendency to want to bring the conversation back to learning, but that risks overlooking what is likely far more important to your child; their standing in their friendship group and the class as a whole.

Modern parents seem to be much more inclined to pay interest in and support their children when it comes to their friendships, but there is a delicate balance to try and maintain. On the one hand, it is vitally important to understand *anything* that is upsetting our children and affecting their learning. Our opinion about how unimportant it is of no use whatsoever. If it affects them then it should be important to us. However, we don't want to meddle too much or too often in the affairs of our little people, for a few reasons:

Firstly, the world of a child moves at a breathtaking pace. You can see the whole spectrum of emotions, from despair to elation, even before they've made it to the school gates. If we insert ourselves too robustly in to a social problem of theirs, we may well do more damage than good in a scenario that would have resolved itself naturally or was fuelled by a passing mood.

Secondly, it would be exhausting to try to keep up with all the twists and turns of their day, week and month. Our adult brains move at a slower pace and trying to keep up with these fleeting thoughts is a bit like watching your kids chase bubbles; they catch very few, and tire quickly.

Finally, and most painfully for us as parents and teachers, they have to learn for themselves. Watching your child so downcast about not being invited to a party or telling you they don't play with anyone at breaktime is truly heartbreaking. We all want nothing more than to sweep in and save the day. I've felt this personally. But consider the message it is sending our children: Mummy or Daddy will fix everything so you don't have to. We all want our children to have the tools to solve their own problems and that means they *have to have problems*.

The best we can do is to act as a filter. Keep the lines of communication open, take an interest in all of these situations and troubles they find themselves in and wait. If a problem persists or begins to cause long-lasting issues then of course we have the option to step in, but pick your moments. You will have a sense of what needs action from you and what doesn't. The message to our child then becomes something akin to: Mummy and Daddy will support and guide you always, but we will only step in and help when you really need it. That fosters true strength, wisdom and saves you chasing too many bubbles.

In the classroom I often see children doubting themselves or looking to their peers to support and agree with their ideas. The problem is that you have young people who are just learning about the world giving advice to other, just as clueless, young people. In my adult life I actually spend a lot of my day feeling just as clueless and confused as I did when I was 10 years old, but at very least I have the benefit of some life experience under my belt which can help me to at least navigate social issues a little better than I did at that age. As parents and teachers, we cannot bestow this kind of life experience on to the children in our care, but what we can do is to let them know it is absolutely normal to feel a little lost. When children have to rely on their peers for guidance, typically the member of their friendship group with the most confidence leads the group. Usually, this person becomes the arbiter of all disputes and the children with less belief in themselves are dragged along by the whims of one particularly strong (or maybe just loud) child. This can cause more problems than you might imagine.

In one of my Year 6 classes, I had a group of seven boys who were all very sporty and appeared to be great friends. Whenever I had spoken to these boys in the years before teaching them, they had all seemed polite and had great energy and enthusiasm. When joining my class, however, they suddenly seemed to be acting a lot more argumentative, resistant to feedback and almost angry most of the time. Now, I understand that when children hit their final year of Primary School, it is natural to become a little more "adolescent" and with that typically comes a bit more attitude. But this somehow didn't feel like that natural consequence of outgrowing primary school. I felt tension within the group and, in one-to-one conversations with these boys, I could still see the polite, well-mannered and positive sides of their personalities that I had witnessed previously. This needed further investigation.

One of the boys, I'll call him Chris, was a lot louder and ostensibly more confident than the rest. He would have an opinion about everything and, whilst usually well-meaning, he would find himself in trouble or annoying others by getting involved in disputes or arguments that had nothing to do with him. Chris was quite used to this role and he was also used to having a few "corrective conversations" with teachers throughout his primary school career. Chris would be quite demanding of the other boys in the group and if anyone stepped out of line they would be shouted down or castigated for not doing what he thought was right.

The other boys, unsure of their social position within the class, tended to follow along in order to stay out of Chris' way. They would add peer pressure to the others and the group became larger and the voices more powerful as they combined.

You might think that as long as they followed Chris' whims, all would be well. But I started to hear more and more reports from parents that their sons just weren't acting the same as before; there was more back-chat at home, more resistance to completing homework and the boys were generally just not fun to be around.

I could see that they were stifling their true personalities in order to fit in and the resistance and anger I could see was not really directed at others, but more at themselves for having to change who they were to stay in the precarious social position they were in.

The easy route, as a teacher or parent, would be to sanction any bad behaviour and chalk it up to "becoming teenage", but this would only serve to cultivate more resentment and resistance from the boys as more relationships suffered. The harder path, but the only true option to solve such a problem, is to tackle the root and be understanding and sympathetic, calling out what I believed the cause of the tension was and taking practical steps to squash it.

Chris's parents didn't believe he was the problem but they could see that even his behaviour had gotten worse. A bit of a dead-end for a teacher as a good relationship with parents makes all the difference, but this result is all-too common, unfortunately.

I spoke to the other boys and their parents separately. For the most part, they all took responsibility for letting their own standards slip but felt that spending more time with Chris and changing their behaviour to be liked or to fit in with him seemed to be the core issue.

Even in the act of having these honest conversations, I could see the weight lift off the boys. They clearly felt seen and understood and this gave them the validation to be honest and help fix the problem. I explained to the boys that I knew what they were really like and I would support them to be that way in the classroom; if they deep down didn't want to play football every lunchtime, I'd assign them to help coach the younger children in their games. If they thought they would like to work in a quiet group during our learning, I'd arrange seat moves or assign them to work with new people on projects. Small changes.

Very quickly, the boys settled back to being their true selves. The effort on my part was minimal: call out what I think the issue was, sympathise, give them the room to change and just tinker around with the classroom setup.

Friendship issues are so wide-ranging you'd be forgiven for thinking that no parent can have the solution to every possible manifestation, and you're right. You can't. But we can take a curious and sympathetic outlook, giving our children room to be kids and express whatever seemingly crazy things they have going on in their heads. The path forward from that will become clear and it is usually very simple, as we have seen in the situation with Chris and his friends.

I also acknowledge that it is easier for a class teacher to get a clear view of friendship issues as they see lots of interactions each day, in many different scenarios from group learning, tests to playtime. As a parent, it is unlikely that you get the opportunity to see the way your child and their friends interact. So, ask them about their friendships instead. I can almost guarantee that a dinner table opening gambit of "How are the girls today? Is everyone getting on?" will garner a fuller response than "What were you learning about in maths today?" Your child might really want to explain a tricky social situation they have recently found themselves in, and you've shown interest and provided the room for them to do that.

They also probably don't want to relive their multiplying fractions learning any more than they have to.

Key lessons:

- To adults they might seem small, but to children, friendship issues have a huge emotional impact.

- Speaking to your child's class teacher will bring awareness of the problem and the teacher will have ways to ease the pressure.

- Don't ask "What did you learn today?" ask about their friends. You'll open up a conversation much more easily.

FAILURE

When I attended primary school in the 1990's, the education system seemed quite satisfied to accept that failing or getting things wrong was just part of the learning process. I remember lots of red pen, crosses to indicate mistakes and the sinking feeling I felt when I read "see me" at the bottom of the page in my exercise book. That meant, quite clearly, that I had missed the point or made a fundamental error and messed up the majority of whatever it was I was learning that day.

As the next lesson began, I would speak to my teacher and they would explain where the gaps in my understanding were and we would both move on. It wasn't necessarily an enjoyable experience, as every child (and adult!) wants to get things correct and feel as if they are progressing. But it never felt excessively painful or as if I was a bad kid for not understanding; I made the error, got taught how to fix it and was a little better the next time.

Parents didn't complain that their child's self esteem was being damaged or as if their souls were being crushed by an oppressive teacher, it was just how teaching worked. I don't think anyone considered there to be any issue with that system of feedback.

When I began training to be a primary school teacher, I realised that a lot had changed in the 30 years since I was at school. Red pens were conspicuously absent, crosses for mistakes had been replaced with dots and the direct "see me" comment was now a list of "next steps". I can't tell you what the motivation was for these changes or name the Government policy that outlawed red pen, but I can tell you one thing: the children still know they've made a mistake.

This softening of feedback terminology and methods does little more than slightly mask what a child already knows: "I got that wrong."

A red cross isn't inherently scary or bad and replacing it with a dot just changes the mark on the paper, not the meaning. A wrong answer is still a wrong answer.

Red pen isn't aggressive or traumatic to read, in fact its contrast to black pen or pencil made it quick for a child to see where they needed to make changes. Writing in purple, pink or green does nothing to change the message.

"Next steps" suggests that a child can build on their learning by following some guidance from the teacher, and there is nothing wrong with this. But if a child has gone off on a tangent and missed some key learning, I'd argue they don't really need "next steps" but rather to retrace a few steps and get the fundamentals right first.

To me, the particular phrase, colour or mark of feedback isn't that important, but the underlying message in school now suggests that we should dance around mistakes and failure as if they are a bad thing. They aren't! Learning simply can't happen unless we push ourselves to a place where we are being challenged and making mistakes to test what we know.

In the 1930's, psychologist Lev Vygotsky described the 'Zone of Proximal Development' – the sweet spot where children learn best with a little help from someone more experienced. This new learning is necessarily beyond what the child currently knows and making mistakes whilst pushing themselves in to new territory is a crucial part of the process. The "more knowledgeable other person" is the class teacher or TA and they, in a perfect world, will be pitching learning that is challenging enough to grasp with enough practice and errors to fully absorb the topic.

A good example from the early stages of Primary school would be addition and subtraction. In Year 1, children will build their knowledge to learn their number bonds to 10; adding numbers to make 10. This is relatively simple as the class can use their fingers to solve any of these calculations. The Zone of Proximal development for a child who knows their number bonds to 10 would be subtraction from 10. A good teacher will show or "model" how to do this, by showing all 10 fingers and putting them down depending on the number to be subtracted. The child will copy and almost always make a few errors before becoming more and more comfortable and independent.

If we keep the learning so simple as to not be a challenge at all, we achieve nothing. As I say to my daughter when she gets frustrated at making errors on her maths homework, "Well I can write out a whole page of the same sum "1+1=" if you like?" Quickly she realises that she wouldn't be learning anything without finding it hard and making mistakes.

I'm not asking for a return to red pen and crosses. Not because I think it will reduce children to quivering messes in every lesson, but because I don't think it matters. What I want is for us as teachers, parents and society to see a mistake and say "Good."

In one of my Year 6 classes, that one word took pride of place in a display above my interactive whiteboard. A black wavy border, white paper background with the word "Good." written in the centre. I credit ex-Navy SEAL Jocko Willink with the idea for this. When leading his troops in Iraq, "Good." Would be his answer to any perceived failure. Why? Because it forced his men to reframe the situation and find a reason why any apparent setback actually helped them. Mistakes were good because you learned.

In my classroom, it was the same. Albeit it with the stakes a little lower than on the battlefield.

"I got my lowest score on my grammar test ever." "Good. Now you know what to revise."

"I didn't get picked to play attack in Hockey." "Good, now you get to try defence and you might be more suited there."

"My group didn't finish our learning in time because we were talking too much and now we need to finish it off in our free time." "Good. I know you'll pick a more focused group next time and you'll probably be more focused too."

It didn't take long before the children in the class knew the answer I might give when a problem arose. I took particular delight when someone would put their hand up in class and tell me a mistake they made, only for another child to gesture toward the big display board and say "Good!" for me. It became a good laugh and nobody took it particularly seriously, which was absolutely the point. It took the sting out of mistakes and turned them in to a mundane part of the process, rather than a judgement about a flaw in your character.

When speaking to your children at home, try tentatively weaving this "Good" mentality through your conversations. The older they are, the more likely they are to believe you are assaulting them with a barrage of toxic positivity in the face of their issues, so you have to sprinkle it in a little delicately at first. However, children adapt quickly and the vast majority of my students has seen the benefit of this reframing approach. At a deeper level it also provides some much-needed relief from the sting of a perceived failure. Labelling a "failed" exam or sports team tryout as "good" will, over time, help both our children and us realise that there is no final moment of judgement. You can always try again, and you get to bring all the lessons you learned with you on the journey. Good.

Key lessons:

- Nobody learns without failing.

- It is a slow process, but we can all embrace failure as the primary driver of growth in our lives if we stop expecting perfection.

- Talk with your child, label each failure as "Good." And decide, honestly, why what happened was a good thing.

CONFIDENCE

If you've read this far, I think it's time for me to reveal a classroom truth to you.

The amount of time and attention your child gets from their teacher is not equal to everyone else.

Maybe you have a more realistic view of the world than I did when I became a teacher, but I wrongly assumed that each of the 30 children in my class would get an equal proportion of my coaching and teaching time. In reality, this just isn't the case.

Now, let me be clear. I know it to be true that each and every teacher wants the best for every child in their class and to treat everyone fairly, but it just doesn't shake out that way.

Within each class exist different "groups". Children with Special Educational Needs (SEN) and Disadvantaged Learners (Children who receive Free School Meals (FSM) or living in care) are the key groups that teachers will focus on in order to support their extra needs. When a teacher takes on a new class, he or she will be made aware of the children from these groups and the extra support which is currently being provided and how to continue this in to the new academic year.

Providing tailored support and more time to teaching children in these groups has benefits for the whole class. For example, extra one-to-one reading time with a Disadvantaged Learner can help that child to close the cognitive gap to their peers by injecting more reading minutes in to their day. With that child's reading skill improving, they can begin to support others near them and contribute more to the group learning they take part in.

SEN encompasses such a broad range of behaviours and support needs that I will address more in a later section, but take a child with Attention Deficit Hyperactivity Disorder (ADHD) for example. As a teacher of someone with ADHD, I know I will have to speak to them shortly after any class activity begins to check that they understand what they need to do and they remember what is expected of them. Naturally, their focus is likely to wane and a quick reminder can keep a child on track. Over the course of a year, those extra check-ins add up, which is why some children naturally get more teacher time than others.

School leadership teams and Governors will quite rightly want to know what is being done in each class to support SEN and DL groups of learners. Data can be gathered and progress checked and reviewed across their primary and secondary school careers. As I've mentioned previously, we know that what gets measured gets actioned, so what of the groups of children who don't fall in to a definable group? What of those who have no diagnosis, no particular economic issues but nevertheless could gain a huge boost from some extra care and attention from the teacher? What about "The Quiet Ones"?

The Quiet Ones – the children who slip under the radar. The 95+% attendance ones. The always remember their PE kit ones. The test scores that meet "Age related expectations" ones. The "I'll work in any group" ones. The "I won't put my hand up but I'll answer a question if I get directly spoken to" ones. The zero behaviour incidents in their whole school career ones.

If this is the first time you've heard of this mythical and unofficial group of children who exist in every classroom and you're wondering whether your child is part of it, here's a good test:

Does your child's class teacher still sometimes get their name wrong, even though it's now the Spring Term and they've been in their class for 5 months? At Open Evening, do you hear more about your child's flawless behaviour record than their learning progress? Do they seem to be passively drifting through their school days, seeming either a little unchallenged or just slightly overlooked?

Now I'm not saying it's a bad thing to be in this group. Not at all. Lots will be learned, targets will get hit, nobody will get offended and overall, the job of the teacher and the school will have been completed to good effect. It just leaves me as a teacher with an uneasy feeling of missed potential. Like buying a Ferrari and only driving it to Sainsburys; yes, you did collect the shopping but you certainly could have gotten more out of your afternoon.

And so many teachers love The Quiet Ones. By the law of averages, if you're spending more time with some students, you have to spend less time with others. I understand that not everyone can or indeed wants to be extroverted and demanding of classroom attention; having a class of 30 students all aggressively vying for the teacher's time would be terrible for all involved. What I am advocating for are these things:

1) The teacher needs to know that your child wants more out of the class or their learning.

2) Your child will likely need to contribute just a small amount more to get outsized positive results.

3) As parents, you also need to have slightly higher expectations of your child's role in the classroom.

The changes I'm suggesting are so small you could quite understandably believe they would have a very weak impact in the classroom. However, I've seen many times what can change with a tiny tweak of an input. Let me give you an example:

In a Year 6 class of mine, I had a boy named Simon. Simon was used to getting good test results and have a fabulous level of general knowledge, supported by his parents who always provided him with new out-of-school experiences and were interested in what was happening in school and how they could support Simon. (If you have an interest in your child's learning like Simon's parents did, I would say you've won half the battle of supporting your child in school, by the way.)

Simon had friends, was polite and was doing really well in everything offered to him in Class 6B. He was still frustrated by our weekly Arithmetic Test, however. This test consisted of 40 quick-fire arithmetic questions to be answered in 30 minutes. It offered very similar questions to those the children would face in their Year 6 SATs exams and the time limit and difficulty of the questions were the same each week. Simon always scored high; 37, 38, even 39 out of 40, but never full marks.

We all knew that Simon that the cognitive horsepower to score full marks. I felt strongly that he was in some way limiting himself.

Simon was known for being quite shy and it was very rare that he would stand up for himself, even when he was well within his rights to do so.

So, at our Parents Open Evening I put the question to Simon, with his mum and dad present:

"Is there any reason why you couldn't be top of the class in maths?"

Simon seemed surprised by the question, as if he had genuinely never considered that he was as good (or better) than the list of Mathematical geniuses he believed were better than him. "I suppose not?" He replied.

Such a seemingly inert question but as I continued talking about his maths skills to mum and dad, I could see that Simon was elsewhere. He really did seem to be imagining himself being the best in the class and this was clearly the first time he had ever been to that place in his mind.

"We'll make a deal then." I said to him when he had come back down to Earth. "You get 40 out of 40 on that test and start considering yourself to be the best in the class at Arithmetic. Why not?"

Simon shook my hand and that ended what I thought was a useful Parent's Open Evening conversation. All of Simon's family were proud of what he was achieving and I was interested to see what happened next.

The very next Friday, as I was slowly disappearing under a pile of Arithmetic papers and completely surrounded by eleven-year-olds throwing them at me, I could hear Simon's voice over the rabble, "Mr B! Mr B! I did it!" His long arm cut through the crowd, brandishing the Arithmetic paper with a big green "40/40" carved in to the front of it.

I could not have been more proud of him. I got up, pouring test papers all over the floor to shake his hand. "That's all you!" I told him.

Simon really seemed to unlock something in his mind in the week leading up to that test and it's my belief that it actually happened instantly, in that Parents' Open Evening conversation when Simon drifted off to another dimension. Just hearing the validation from his teacher that he could be the best allowed him to put himself there and it took the brakes off once and for all. Again, my teaching was no better and I didn't teach Simon anything profound within that week, he had just allowed his confidence to grow a tiny bit, with outsized results.

As a teacher, I'm not interested in whether it's a test result, a dance recital, some handwriting, or scoring your first goal in our Hockey PE sessions, it doesn't matter to me. I'm here to notice where your potential isn't meeting your outcomes and to help you get there. You decide where "there" is and what's important to you. As a parent of a school-age child, is there somewhere you feel like your child is somehow holding the brakes on a little bit, even if they don't know it? Hopefully my example of Simon demonstrates how little it takes to support a child towards a big breakthrough.

Simon's example falls under number 1 – **"Your teacher needs to know your child wants more out of the class or their learning."** If it appears to the teacher that the child and parents are completely satisfied with how things are going in school, then it is unlikely that the teacher will proactively look to shake things up. It is a teacher's job to notice these gaps and they will do it without a nudge, but it is much less likely than if you make you or your child's desire to better, known.

On to number 2:

"Your child will likely need to contribute just a small amount more to get outsized positive results."

In order to build confidence in class, it will take a little bit of extra effort from your child. But I truly do mean a little bit of effort. I'm not suggesting it is necessary for wholesale personality transplant in to a fire-breathing extrovert for your child to be more successful and confident in class.

Andy is an example of what happens when this second element isn't met. Andy was a student in one of my Year 6 classes. As one of the oldest in the class, Andy had clearly taken advantage of the extra days in school that comes with being born early in the academic year; in fact, if Andy was born just a week earlier than he was he would have been in the year above and in secondary school at that time. He had no problem with meeting the expected standards of Year 6 learning, but even he would admit he was hitting these targets at a canter and not really stretching himself. Upon speaking with Andy's parents, they felt frustrated that he wasn't seeming to be challenged or meeting his full potential, and I agreed.

Andy had a particular "style" in lessons. When a maths session began, he would pay the minimum attention required and then complete the required learning. He would then grind to a complete halt and just talk to his friends. When reminded that there were other activities to complete, and *only* then, Andy would complete the further activities and call it a day. It was like leading a grumpy thoroughbred racehorse around a field by the reins; we both knew he could take off and show the world something special, but he would rather be led slowly around and do the bare minimum to get to the next break. Andy's test scores were good but he was unchallenged and bored. It was a great start that his parents wanted to discuss his potential and how we could meet it but the fact was that Andy himself was just not interested in pushing himself to the limit.

I don't think this is Andy's fault, necessarily. As his teacher, I take full responsibility for not being able to find the key to enthusing him or inspiring him to want more from his learning. That's a lock that I regrettably could not open in the year I spent as his teacher. I find that endlessly frustrating and it does truly fuel me to want to become a better judge of character and to become more insightful to children's needs so that those missed opportunities don't come up as much, but they do happen.

It goes to show why element number 2 - "Your child will likely need to contribute just a small amount more to get outsized positive results." - is actually crucial. Andy wasn't interested in this and as such, he did well in primary school but he left some progress on the table and that's a shame. I have a feeling that he will be very successful in secondary school and it's quite possible he just hasn't yet found the topic or subject that really sparks his drive to know more and be the best he can be.

In general, all I want to see is the child in the class giving a little bit more. I mean putting their hand up to answer a question once more per *week* to start with. I mean sitting down to complete an early morning activity instead of talking for 5 more minutes. I mean selecting focused people instead of your best mates for a group project. I mean asking the teacher one follow-up question about something they didn't understand, even writing a question in their learning book for the teacher to see would be a fantastic start.

Confidence in the classroom is closely linked to identity. In most UK schools, children stay with the same group of around 30 children in their class from Year 1 to Year 6. In most cases this is because the school is "one form entry"; meaning that there is a single class of each year and therefore there would be nowhere to switch to. But many schools have multiple classes per year and yet switching between classes is very rare; usually reserved for cases of bullying or some kind of longer-term issue which a parent or the school feel might be rectified by a class switch.

This means that the in-class hierarchy is typically formed quite early in a class's journey through the school and it doesn't change as much as you might imagine. The loudest and most confident children will put their hands up regularly in Year 1 and the class seem to become used to the same 5-10 children answering questions. This works well for all involved as the children who enjoy interacting more with the teacher get to do that and the children who would prefer to shy away from answering questions have a solid cohort of confident children to rely on to break the silence and keep the lessons moving when the teacher poses a problem or wants input from the class.

However, the relatively fixed nature of the class dynamic isn't really optimal for all. A child who is quiet in Year 2 but really develops their ability as a writer might have some brilliant ideas but their identity as one of the quieter children might make them feel like they can't break the mould and offer their ideas. As adults, we might be inclined to feel this is a bit silly; if someone has a good idea it should be shared! I totally agree, but the power of subconscious peer pressure and class identity is a more powerful force than one might imagine.

Clearly, it is a teacher's job to tease out these good ideas and make sure they are aired. Good learning should be shared and celebrated. One way I do this is to very gradually raise a child's profile in the class.

In a year 5 class of mine was a girl who spent every spare minute reading. Thankfully, this is a relatively common sight in a primary school as reading is championed by all staff and more minutes spent with a book in hand really does translate in to better learning outcomes across the board. Helena was in a league of her own, though. She would take a book out on the playground; reading everything from fantasy stories to Norse mythology. She was clearly absorbing the vocabulary, structure and flow of what she was reading as her own creations in class were packed with interesting twists and turns and character development far beyond her years. But Helena was "one of the quiet ones". Her class identity was that of a polite, hard-working person but not someone who shared their ideas.

Upon reading a particularly fascinating passage as I passed her table one day, I asked Helena if she would like to share it with the class. Her eyes widened with dread at the very thought of it and all I got in response was a vigorous shake of the head. Fair enough, I thought, I don't want anyone to feel embarrassed. But this had to be shared. "Can I read it for you then?" I asked her. I can't be sure, but I felt like I detected a sliver of excitement and pride from Helena at the idea of this. I feel she knew very well that she had created something brilliant but she just didn't have the confidence to be the person to share it and face what she perceived to be the silent scrutiny of her classmates.

I took Helena's book to the front and read through the passage. I didn't say it was Helena's book – in the melee of a writing lesson I had been around most tables and nobody had noticed that Helena's book was missing from her desk. The paragraph I read could have easily come from a published story. Every word was carefully selected and I myself could learn a lot from the way she had described the setting of a post-apocalyptic city.

There were audible gasps from others in the class and as I finished, I revealed it was Helena's learning and initiated a round of applause which the rest of the class enthusiastically joined in with. Helena looked terrified, relieved and proud all at once. In that moment, without her really knowing it, her class identity had shifted. Helena had now ascended to "reluctant star author".

That nudge out of her comfort-zone built momentum over time. Helena gradually began to read some of her own writing in class and in the coming months I gave her a class award for her writing, again sharing a short passage from one of our lessons. This time the whole school was able to witness her ability and the fruits of her passionate reading habit. The acknowledgement of the teachers and other classes gave Helena the belief in herself that had been previously limited by her class identity.

An academic year can feel like a long time and as a parent you could rightfully assume that the teacher will have enough time to read and influence the class identity by the time they finish teaching in the summer. In many cases they will but I know from personal experience that I can't always help children to reach their full potential in those 11 months. There are general patterns which seem to occur year on year and will help to illustrate why some children don't get the full opportunity to shift their identity.

Autumn Term – In the UK this relates to the two terms between September and the Christmas break. The class teacher is starting from zero knowledge about the class, getting to know them and their apparent strengths and weaknesses.

Spring Term – This spans the two terms between January and the Easter break. In this term, the class teacher will be getting to know the children and beginning to push them towards their potential. Bear in mind that there will be emerging Special Educational Needs (SEN) that the teacher will need to support, along with revision for assessments such as SATs in Year 2 and Year 6.

Summer Term – Between Easter and the end of the academic year is the Summer Term. The class teacher will know the children well and be able to most precisely guide each student towards maximising their learning and identifying their true strengths.

It would take somewhat of a superhuman teacher to inherit a class and be able to spot and make progress towards building a child's class identity in the Autumn Term. It does happen but I would say it is rare. Everyone is settling in to the new routines and more challenging learning of the class and the general theme is "Where are we?" – This is an information gathering period of time for children and teacher alike.

More progress can be made in Spring term and the class teacher will be making changes, sorting friendship dynamics and challenging individual children to do more, share more and push a little more. The Spring Term, as mentioned, is typically the busiest time for class assessments and this can take the focus away from challenging individuals to try new things.

Summer term provides an excellent opportunity for development and, if handled correctly, the teacher will have facilitated a route to a child's class identity being completely transformed. I have seen so many examples of a child ending the academic year with a completely different role in our class group and being fully accepted as almost a new person entirely! This is so heartening to witness, yet it typically comes at the end of the year; just before you have to faithfully hand your class to a new teacher or, in the case of Year 6, a completely new school. It's daunting for everyone involved and one can hope you've done enough to equip each child with the best opportunity to take their "new" class identity and have the strength of character to continue to act and behave with more faith in themselves and not retreat towards their old comfort zone that took so much time and support to break out of.

Key lessons:

- A child's role in the class is never fixed. They might be one of "The Quiet Ones" now, but that can change.

- Get the class teacher on board. They can make changes that will make it easier for your child to speak up more and boost their own confidence.

- Nobody expects an overnight transformation. Small changes add up.

- Low confidence is a limiting belief. That glass ceiling can be broken and it can lead to real success.

RESILIENCE

Resilience is the ability to continue in the face of difficulties. It is such a buzz word of modern life that I was reluctant to use it as the title for this chapter, but regardless of the fact that we use this word so much, I believe it is an attribute that we all want and we also want to instil it in our children.

For years I've absorbed book after book on personal development and ways to build resilience. I've found great comfort in learning about how to reframe difficult situations, take things less personally, meditate to allow emotions to surface and be processed and all kinds of techniques that are reported to help me or anyone else weather a difficult time. I believed that if I absorbed enough of this content then, when life threw one of its curveballs, I would be able to deploy a tactic from a book I have read and shrug it off, barely losing stride in my journey to complete self-mastery.

But that isn't how it works in reality.

I've learned resilience isn't stored up for later – it's built in the very moment you endure difficulty. As you are feeling the pain of illness, job loss, relationship troubles or anything in between, life doesn't stop for you to catch your breath, gather your faculties and get yourself together. You still have to go to work, try to be kind to the people around you and get your children to school.

If that sounds overwhelming, it's because it really is. However, as you drag yourself through your work day whilst your head is spinning about test results, that argument you had with your husband or your child's poor school behaviour, something inside of you is alchemising. Often you don't feel as if any progress is being made; as if you've been dealt a bad hand and somehow you should have foreseen what was going to happen so you could dodge the issue before it hit you, but life throws punches you can't always dodge.

As I get older, I realise that every person and every family is carrying burdens of considerable weight. Despite appearances on social media, nobody gets out of this life without a few scars. As a teacher I get to see behind the curtain of hundreds of family situations as I learn about them from the children themselves.

Firstly, you should be assured that whilst in school, your son or daughter is being looked after well and in the vast majority of cases, listened to by their teacher or TA. You don't need to have that extra worry hanging over your head when you're already struggling to get your head around whatever else it is you're facing.

Despite the best efforts of parents, children will absorb every word you say and if you aren't saying it explicitly, the "feel" of your household. Children are so sensitive to an atmosphere of tension or worry that it is impossible to fully shield them from the emotional impact of a difficult time for the family.

That isn't necessarily a bad thing. As parents we know that one of our key jobs is to gently guide our children from a world of complete innocence to helping them to understand that the world isn't all teddies and cartoons. Ideally, we would want that to be a gradual process in which we have the time and space to discuss each new revelation of the "real" world. When should you have the "Father Christmas" conversation? When should they learn about boyfriends and girlfriends? When should they learn that feeling happy isn't usually the default emotion of anyone? Those are all choices we have to make without much of a roadmap and none of us want our children to experience a traumatic event in the name of "building resilience", but if they should see Mummy cry when she's feeling grief is that such a bad thing?

You can imagine a spectrum, with the left side being "Complete innocence and denial" and the right side labelled "Unfiltered reality". We know that it would be overwhelming for a five-year-old to learn about war and despair, but we can also imagine how damaging it would be for a child to be preserved in a world of false innocence for so long that this veneer is liable to be cracked without warning when another child reveals the Christmas secret or they begin to feel shame for not feeling happy all the time. We aim to guide our children along that spectrum from left to right as they grow and mature their understanding of the world.

Each difficult scenario or test of resilience is an opportunity for parents and teachers to compassionately peel away another wafer-thin layer of protection and help the child to learn that bad things do happen but they will be fine anyway, with our help.

In the classroom, between (and sometimes during) teaching, I'm also a fixer of a multitude of mini concerns from the children. Here are some high-frequency examples:

- "She's looking at me funny and winding me up."
- "He's leaving me out in games and I have no-one to play with."

- "They're whispering and I know it's about me."
- "She said my bag/hair/shoes looked weird/odd/stupid."

As a new teacher and at the beginning of my career not yet a parent, my instinctive reaction was to politely dismiss these concerns with a "Oh I'm sure they didn't mean it." response. These worries seemed so small and insignificant that it seemed like a truly impossible mission to teach a day of lessons and firefight every comment or look. It probably *is* an impossible task to deal with all of these worries, but at lunch one day I was recalling my own school life. I still remember the muttered comments about my acne or the way my hair looked. If I still remember that after 25 years then these comments, although seemingly trivial when viewed through adult's eyes, have impact.

Think back yourself about your primary or secondary school days. I would guess within 30 seconds you will be able to recall at least one stinging comment from a classmate. You might even feel a slight flush of adrenaline and embarrassment as you remember that classroom, hallway or sports field where it hit you. Those comments are still locked up in there and if they are there for us as adults then we need to take our children's concerns seriously and help them to realise that we understand how it feels. This is a huge part of helping them to build resilience.

Life happens and we should *want* our children to experience everything; the good and the bad. But more than anything, we need to ride those waves with them, acknowledge that comments hurt and sometimes they will go through an event that strips away a layer of their innocence before they and you are ready for it. Show an interest in every part of their world, however trivial it may seem to you as an adult. You will learn something new and much more importantly, if you're there to listen for the small problems then they will trust you with the big ones, too. You may not feel that commiserating with a 9-year-old about the reality of the Tooth Fairy is necessary, but if it's important to them then it's important.

Key lessons:

- If it's important to your child, it's important.

- As parents and teachers, we should strive to a safety net to the children we care for, but not smothering.

- Resilience can only be built by going through difficult times. Similar to failure, it feels bad at the time but can lead to great things.

PART II

SUBJECT SPECIFIC SUPPORT

The post-school debrief with a child is notorious for lacking in detail. Like a spy under interrogation, they give away the bare minimum whilst appearing to comply. Finding out what happened in maths is like asking for the nuclear warhead launch codes. I will, however, stick to the key theme of this book and invite us all to give the kids a break.

In endeavouring to engage children and to be able to regularly check in on progress, most lessons in modern schools have many "parts". You may well be used to a much simpler structure in your own school days, I certainly am. In the 1990s, I recall a lesson being broken in to three main sections:

1. Teacher input (being taught something new)
2. Children practised on a worksheet
3. Short summary and end of lesson.

Maybe lessons really were that simple, or maybe my 7-year-old brain just made them seem that way. Either way, it doesn't really matter.

A modern maths lesson's parts now look broadly like this:

1. Recall previous learning linked to today's lesson
2. Children respond to the teacher's marking or feedback from the previous session.
3. Warm-up activity (general maths skills like arithmetic)
4. Short teacher input
5. Activity to check understanding
6. Second input to challenge those who are confident and support those who didn't grasp the new concept first time around
7. Children work on their own activities, tailored to their attainment level on that day
8. Summary and knowledge check

9. Children give self-generated feedback on their performance.

All of these individual parts are backed by research and all have a positive impact on the retention of information over time, it just seems that with so many moving parts in each individual lesson, it is difficult for a child to distil an answer to the question, "What did you learn in maths today?"

In my experience, this added complexity in the structure of lessons is easy for the children to grasp but trickier for the teachers to keep up with. Once I have started a lesson, I won't sit down in my seat until the end: checking understanding, grabbing tailored resources for various groups, giving live feedback and answering questions all contribute to both a well-delivered lesson and also my 10 to 15 thousand steps I would take in a working day.

"SCHEMES"

No, not the latest plot to carve out some time to wet tissue paper and weld it to the ceiling of the boys' toilets, but the (generally paid for) content of lessons which cover the National Curriculum topics for an academic year.

Building a scheme in-house would take a mammoth amount of extra work for teachers so schools typically buy a package for each subject which maps out objectives and teaches the children in a systematic and hopefully entertaining manner. Schools will typically buy a scheme for maths, writing and reading but there is purchasable content for every conceivable lesson at every level.

My experiences of schemes are generally good and there is no doubt that they achieve their aim of curriculum coverage. However, different schools within a connected group or "Trust" might select different schemes from one another and the benefits of one scheme over another are often debated, leading to frequent changes and shifts for teachers to keep up with. Therefore, it would be of no use for me to provide guidance about how to support your child in any specific scheme as there is a strong probability that you will a) never have heard of it and b) the scheme will have changed by the time you understand it. In this section, then, I will give guidance around the core 'Unchangeables': the pillars of learning in each subject that will always be relevant and provide the greatest benefit to understanding. For example, regardless which maths scheme is flavour of the year, children will have to know their times tables, be able to summarise a text and be able to create a story of their own. It is my aim to equip you with some basic tools to help you support your child and not get caught up in the changing tides of policy and new ideas which are all subject to change at a moment's notice.

READING

In UK schools, "Open Evening" typically happens three times per year, once for each of the Autumn, Spring and Summer terms. Each family has the opportunity to book an incomprehensibly short amount of time to discuss their child's progress with the teacher. In the early terms, these meetings can be limited to as little as five minutes in length. This is to enable every family to fit in on one day without the session turning in to some kind of overnight academic endurance event, but to me this amount of time barely allows for the initial greetings before you're getting ready to wrap up. Necessarily then, any complaints or comments need to be refined to single-sentence sound bites that the teacher can acknowledge, record or even attempt to deal with in the 300 second window.

One of the most common snippets I hear is "I just can't get them to read!" Much as I and the parents might like, changing a child's outlook towards reading is not something I can do in that amount of time, but it certainly highlights that passion for reading is lacking in many families.

In any class there are at least a few very keen readers; like Helena and others I mentioned in a previous chapter. Parents have a natural inclination to notice the other children in school, usually from a perspective of "I hope my child isn't falling behind." So, when they look through the classroom window at pick up time and see a cohort of children serenely flicking through the latest Harry Potter book whilst their child is throwing their school bag at someone, the tendency is to internalise this and see it as some kind of parenting failure. It isn't.

I'd like everyone to read more as I know how closely this extra effort translates in to academic success, but we have to be tactful in how we try to cultivate any new habit with our children: any parent who has tried to enforce a 30 minute per day reading routine will know that you'll almost always be met with strong resistance to anything that feels like extra learning.

Before I explain how I've managed to increase children's weekly reading time, I should detail the different skills within reading and why it is one of the habits you shouldn't give up on.

In school, reading ability is broadly broken in to Decoding, Inference and Comprehension. We can't understand a story or text if we don't understand how to sound out the words so Decoding naturally comes at the beginning of our learning journey. You will have heard about Phonics and this is the teaching of how to break down a word in to its constituent parts and say it properly. Whilst Phonics learning is a huge focus in early school years and it somewhat assumed to be fully understood from around Year 3 onwards, the English language is tricky to grasp for older children, too. Take the following list of words:

- Through
- Rough
- Bough
- Cough
- Thought

Each of these words contains the group of letters "ough" but in each this group of letters is pronounced differently. Understanding this is a matter of practice and as adults we read these words without issue, but when we have to explain this to a child we can sympathise with the difficulty they might face with the odd rules of our language.

Phonics teaching in primary schools is typically very good and you will notice your child becoming more confident in using these new sounds as they progress through the school year. In order to support them at home, consider buying a set of Phonics cards and learning the associated rhymes or sentences the school use in their teaching. For example, the sound "ow" is supported with the sentence "Ow brown Cow". Compare this with "Ow blow the snow." to see the difference. When reading with younger children, knowing these phrases can be very helpful as you will be reinforcing what the school is teaching and your child gets a chance to educate you at the same time. Trust me, get one of those little ditties wrong and you'll certainly be corrected, usually with a tone of complete contempt for your ignorance.

Inference is the skill of understanding a story and being able to explain what has happened and what might happen in the future. It includes being able to deduce what a character is feeling by how they act. Your child may be able to read, "The man's face went bright red and he clenched his fists." But can they infer that the man is angry?

Thankfully, developing Inference skills can be done with the use of one simple question:

"How do you know?"

Parent: "How is the man feeling?"

Child: "Angry I think."

Parent: "How do you know?"

Child: "Because it says his face is red and that's what happens when you're angry. And he's squeezing his hands like what I do when you try to get me to read every night."

Parent: "Great, you've got it."

Sneakily add this question in whilst watching cartoons and you will quickly help to boost your child's understanding of Inference. Ask them to predict what might happen next, or to retell a Bluey episode. It might take longer than the episode itself, but it builds the skill.

Comprehension is the ability to read words, process them and understand their meaning. Once a child can decode each part of a word and say them, they can technically "read" a story, but without comprehension they won't have understood what is happening. It is certainly a higher-level skill than decoding but it is taught from the beginning of primary school and its importance in all learning cannot be overstated.

We can all agree that we want our children to be able to understand what they read, but the term "comprehension" can seem vague and difficult to teach. It is more straightforward to view comprehension as a collection of skills that work together to form an overall understanding.

Being able to summarise a piece of text or a story is a key part of comprehension. From the very first books children read in school, they will be asked the same follow-up question, "Can you tell me what happened in the story?" This is used as a key diagnosis question to elicit whether the child has understood what they have read, or whether they are just decoding the words in an effort to finish the book.

In these early stages of learning how to read, children can have wildly varying abilities in both decoding and comprehension. At age 5, my daughter Connie could decode most words and was flying through books. My other daughter, Immy, would skip and guess words that seemed to fit. It seemed as if Connie was progressing well and that Imogen was a little slower to grasp the subject. But ask Connie what the story was about and she would struggle to comprehend the themes or be able to summarise the book. At times, Immy would overhear her reading and she would shout out what the meaning of the book was, even though she hadn't read a word of it (much to Connie's frustration). It was at this point I noticed that Connie needed much more focus on her comprehension and, whilst Immy would creatively switch words that she couldn't decode, she always seemed to understand what had happened. Don't falsely assume, as I did, that reading speed correlates with understanding; ask challenging questions and you will quickly see where your child needs extra help.

Once a child is used to being able to summarise a story, you can begin to work on another facet of comprehension: prediction.

As adults, we know the skilled predictors as they are the people who manage to ruin every TV drama with an insightful yet suspense-destroying comment like, "I bet she's pregnant." "I reckon he's an undercover cop." "I think he's dead too, that's why he can see dead people like that boy."

(Hopefully) without realising it, our box-set companions are comprehending everything they are watching and generating possible future scenarios before they happen. As parents, we have the opportunity to help build the next generation of annoying partners by simply pausing whilst reading a book and asking "What do you think happens next?" In that moment where you stop, your child has to recall the story, summarise it quickly and generate a plausible future event. This is a high-level skill and certainly worth building at a young age.

I would suggest that you give your child a chance to think for at least seven seconds before helping them. This is to give them a chance to complete all of the mental gymnastics I just mentioned and not rush to guess an answer. Life in general seems to require an instant answer for every question, so building in more processing time for every request of your child helps to keep them regulated and not feel panicked in to snatching at the first idea that pops in their head.

If seven seconds isn't enough, or your child's comprehension skills still need a little work, then we can make use of the beautiful illustrations in most books we read to our kids. Hold the page you're pausing on and quickly flick to the next page to give them a sneak peek at the next event, then slip back to the original page. They can then add this new information to their "guess" and this can help reading feel a little more fun while they learn those prediction skills in the background.

In the classroom I would often ask the children to predict what might happen next in our class story. Regardless of the theme of the book, and likely more out of hope than expectation, many of the boys would predict some kind of huge firefight with machine guns or rampaging dinosaurs. Maybe I should have predicted it wasn't a good idea to ask.

If the technical aspects of teaching children don't read don't appeal to you (and I can quite understand why they wouldn't) then there is a much more straightforward way to support your child's development in this area.

Research shows that children learn just as much from observation of others than they do from being verbally told what to do. (Waterman 2017) Fittingly, I learned this lesson as a parent whilst observing my daughters playing on a Saturday morning. I had woken up early, sorted breakfast, checked social media, tidied the house up a bit, checked emails and sent a few messages to friends about weekend plans. Shortly afterward, the girls started playing a new game, a game where they wandered about on mobile phones; calling and texting each other and their friends and not doing much else.

On some level, we all know we should be using our phones less and being more present around our children. But if you're anything like me you're also a leading expert in how to rationalise that behaviour if you are a little bit addicted:

"I just had to send an email quickly."

"Sorry girls I'm just messaging Scott. I'll be with you in one minute."

You can add your own examples, and doing so will probably reveal how weak your reasons are for being on your phone and maybe even help you to realise that you are scrolling too much. But nothing hits home quite like seeing a five- and six-year-old roleplaying constant phone use in front of you on a Saturday morning. I've begun to erode their attention span before they've even turned a real device on!

I would love to tell you that that was the point in which I instantly jettisoned my phone from my life, committing to a complete off-grid lifestyle. It wasn't, but I have reduced my phone time around the kids and it led me to trialling reading more as the next behaviour to be imitated.

I have always enjoyed reading, but since the creation of the dopamine fruit machine that is the smartphone, I (like many others) have found it harder to start reading and maintain my focus for a long period. I had plenty of books I was yet to start so I began to switch phone time for book time at home. It is truly fascinating how quickly it works. It certainly wasn't instant but my daughters started to use their own books in roleplay and would quite often come and sit next to me with a book whilst I was reading. I couldn't believe quite how effective just reading for 15 minutes would be on their behaviour. It made me think about the effect of every behaviour they see from me, but I decided to park that and deal with one shortcoming at a time.

How much are you reading at home? Try not to rationalise in the same way I have with phone use, citing having no time or not being able to find an interesting book: if we're using these excuses, we can't really blame our children for using the same lines when we are trying to get them to read more either.

Find a book that you might be interested in. It doesn't have to be long, profound or critically acclaimed but if you are stuck then pick one of the top 10 in the fiction or non-fiction charts depending on your general preference, and commit to reading for 15 minutes per day. I'm not asking you to performatively stroll in to your child's bedroom brandishing a copy of Hamlet, just take some time out to get a break from your phone and build your own attention span back to a healthy state. See what your children do.

I appreciate that my sample size for my initial "reading imitation experiment" was a little small, so I took it to the classroom.

Each day, when the children got back in from lunch, they have around 15 minutes of silent time. Many already read, some colour, some tidy their drawers. A decent minority try to silently communicate with their friends throughout this time, comically pretending to read a book when I look up at the class. Most of the time, I would be preparing resources for the final lesson of the day, stapling learning on to a display board and generally circulating the classroom. For a couple of weeks, I committed to silently reading as they came back in to class and continuing for those 15 minutes.

Again, the results really impressed me. The number of children reading in the class went up. The number of people pretending to read went down. There were less distractions and the silence was held because there were now fewer people to try and have a silent conversation with as they were *actually* reading.

More heartening than all of this was that the children took a genuine interest in what I was reading. At the time, it was the fantastic *I May Be Wrong* by Bjorn Nattihko Lindeblad. It opened a few interesting conversations about meditation, mindfulness and career choices.

All this goes to show that it may only require a small habit change for you to inspire your children to read. I have seen the effects for myself and even if it doesn't work for you, you get to cut down on your screen time a bit. Don't worry, I won't judge you if you pick up your phone as this is the end of the chapter.

Key lessons:

- Children copy what they see; if you aren't reading much, they won't either.

- At any age, you can read to your children. This boosts confidence and you can start a good book together.

- Build reading ability by asking smart questions like, "How do you know?" when your child makes a statement about something they've read.

- There is a difference between being able to read words and understanding what you have read. Learn your child's reading weaknesses so you learn how to support them.

WRITING

I've always found it interesting that of all the subjects that parents ask for advice about, writing is mentioned the least. It has an almost mysterious quality, as if we assume that the ability to write stories or answer questions leans more towards an innate ability rather than a malleable skill we can develop.

Like reading, the skills of writing are used throughout all subjects and are less topic-based than learning maths. We learn to use capital letters and full stops when writing about science, philosophy and everything in between. Even our maths tests require explanations and reasoning as to how an answer has been reached. There are a lot of moving parts which combine to form a child's writing style, so knowing which lever to pull can be difficult to identify.

Every child is taught grammar rules, how to use punctuation, how to spell appropriate words for their age group and how to join their handwriting. On top of this, there is a growing expectation of creativity and writing flair across different text types. Typically, when the class teacher is focusing on one of these elements, another worsens. We play literary whack-a-mole and hope that, as the school years go by, more and more of these skills become automatic and our pool of remaining learning targets gets smaller and the creases become easier to iron out.

That learning journey works well for most children, but if a child fails to grasp the basics, such as how to use a comma appropriately, then as the learning becomes more challenging, they can find themselves weighed down with a feeling of "falling behind" as they try to juggle how to use rhyming couplets in poetry *and* correcting those grammatical errors at the same time. This is a frustrating difference compared to maths learning, where a child can struggle with a topic, percentages for example, but know that even if they don't understand it well, soon the lessons will move on to another area of maths that they have a better chance of understanding. Writing skill builds on itself and requires a breadth of attention that can be hard to keep working in sync.

What writing looks like in school

In each academic year, children will get the opportunity to learn to write different text types. The one we all remember from school is a narrative; a story. This text type is usually considered to be the most enjoyable because the technical requirements are more relaxed; you are encouraged to be creative and allow your own style to flow. Other text types include recounts (such as newspaper reports), poetry, instructions and reports.

The best method I've seen and used for teaching writing is to model some writing in the style of the current text type on the board and then allow the children to write their own version of it. If the teacher talks through their thinking, "Hmm, what other word could I use for 'angry' here?" etc, then the children begin to understand that each and every word should be carefully selected by the author.

Once they have a solid collection of these adapted sentences, they can use these as a framework for their own piece of writing or, if confident, decide to go off-piste and write their own original version.

When supporting your child at home, speak aloud your thinking about the words used in a sentence. Useful phrases include:

- "I want to use a word that means _ _ _ _ _ but is more interesting."
- "Which verb or "doing word" could I put here?"
- "What do I need to remember for the start and end of a sentence?" (capital letters and full stops)

By sprinkling in slightly more technical jargon and reminding them of basic writing protocol, these routines will become more embedded for when they come to write independently.

Spelling lessons are usually placed at the beginning of a writing lesson and it is a skill that is practiced little and often. Spelling is a source of frustration for many, not just for those who feel there might be a clinical issue such as dyslexia present in their child or themselves. No doubt, it is a facet of writing that is harder to improve than learning grammar rules or what an adverbial is, but there are some simple strategies to help.

Firstly, review your child's understanding of Phonics. Remembering the phrase "Coat in a boat" will help your child to remember the sound that the "oa" pairing can make and cause them to try using this when spelling new words that contain that sound, such as "bloated". Phonics is now taught up to Year 6 (the end of primary school) as educators realise the true value of understanding sounds in language. There are many websites and guides online that can provide you with lists of these rhymes, or ask the class teacher for an aide memoire.

Handwriting is still taught as a short standalone lesson but it is important to remember, if handwriting is causing frustration, that typing on a keyboard is the primary way of writing in the modern world. We cannot discard it as a skill entirely, but its value is certainly diminishing. Further, most handwriting improves with practice and time alone. It is more easily improved when focused on early in school, but taking 5 minutes a day on letter formation can and does have a noticeable positive impact.

Grammar lessons standalone and happen in between writing sessions. They usually focus on one or two topics, such as adverbs or when to use a semi-colon. As with "normal" writing lessons, children are shown how to use each tool and then progress to including them in their independent writing. More often than not, they seem to be forgotten as soon as the bell goes for the end of the lesson, but I can sympathise; I still have to teach myself what the "subjunctive form" is before I begin that particular class each year.

Teaching writing at primary school and early secondary school level can seem formulaic, and it is. Before a child can begin to create pieces of writing that have flair and personality, they need to deeply understand the building blocks that provide the foundation for exceptional writing.

Each school's writing scheme and the National Curriculum will ensure that each of these building blocks are taught and build in complexity as the school years progress. It is the job of the class teacher to notice which aspects of writing each child is finding difficult, but parents can assist too.

Once children know how to form sentences and they have a concept to write about, I guide them to keep their narrative balanced by asking them to move between Action and Description as they move down their page.

In the first half of primary school, teachers will have to tightly control what each child is writing about to ensure they stay focused on getting the basics correct. In the second half of primary school and beyond, children will have much more narrative freedom and can create their own stories that have a few restrictions. Often, the teacher will define the setting or the characters involved, so that children don't have to create everything from scratch. Other times, teachers will insist on children adding different literary devices, such as alliteration or fronted adverbials, in order that the children can use these as evidence that they can use these devices accurately.

All this sounds wonderfully wholesome until the machine guns and aliens arrive.

Naturally, when released from the shackles of their younger years, children will delight in their newly-acquired freedom as an author. Almost without fail, this will result in every story culminating in a hail of automatic weapon fire and death on a genocidal scale. From experience, this does seem to be more of a male trait, but not exclusively. Either way, these stories create an excellent teaching point.

As they descend from their euphoric state, these young writers quickly realise that more guns do not equal a better story. Endings in which every living thing dies leave no satisfying conclusion to most and the children realise that an Action-dominant style leaves a lot to be desired. Most of the time, it isn't even clear where the carnage has taken place, as, lost in their writing frenzy, the author hasn't given any setting description at all.

Over time, we can begin to insist on adding a phase of action (guns optional) and then a phase of setting and character description. This can be repeated until this structure forms something more like a story from a book.

The alternative route in early "free" writing is the Description-dominant path. Some children take great pleasure in weaving words into a rich and living world, full of unique and lifelike characters. Characters whom end up doing very little.

Paragraph after paragraph are carefully written but what remains at the end of the session is more akin to a static piece of art than a journey.

For these children, it is helpful to support them in writing a short bullet-point plan of events for their story. Even just one action for the beginning, a "problem" of some sort for the characters to solve and then, most challenging, an ending.

Description-dominant writers seem to find is easier to get the balance correct more quickly, as they naturally want their characters to do more, they just don't know how to get there. The bullet-point plan is a sure-fire way to help them create better stories.

So read a piece of independent writing that your child has created. I promise it will be very quickly apparent which of these styles they are leaning toward. Help them create a plan for each section of heir story; whether that be a mandatory setting description to start, or a few action waypoints to keep the story interesting.

Through writing this book, I have truly absorbed some guidance I tell the children in my class: writing is never really "finished". As Stephen King said about editing, "Only God gets it right first time..." Nobody should expect to be able to produce a piece of writing that is flawless on the first pass. It isn't possible and we should instead show our children that making changes is an essential part of the writing process. It isn't "wrong", it could just be improved.

Helpfully, writing tasks in school have a defined time limit that offer a hard deadline to the creation of each piece of writing. This allows the children to move on easily because they simply have to, although I can't help but wonder what we could produce if each young person could continue to refine one story over the whole course of an academic year.

Writing is a journey of patience and persistence. If we can help our children to see writing as a way to experiment with new ideas and share their voice, then I believe they will be more inclined to learn the commas, clauses and colons that bring their imagination to life on the page.

Key lessons:

- Writing combines many moving parts: spelling, handwriting, grammar and planning.

- Children often lean toward being action-dominant or description-dominant.

MATHS

As I remember, maths in primary school seemed to be counting lots of colourful pictures and some basic arithmetic. Upon starting my teacher training and studying the curriculum, I realised that either my memory is much worse than I thought it was or I have just repressed the memories having to learn Fractions, Percentages and Decimals at eight years old.

I remember enjoying maths at primary school and that was due to a combination of good teaching and because I found it to be relatively manageable. Viewing it now from a teacher's perspective, I can completely understand why learning maths in school seems to be a sticking point for children and a cause of frustration for parents when trying to assist with learning or homework.

There are a two main reasons for this, the first is specificity. Whereas the skill of reading is being used in all lessons as a child has to read and understand text to engage with any subject, each maths topic is its own silo; requiring a unique skill be recalled and deployed to answer each question and progress. One day it's calculating 35% of 400, the next day it's multiplying 520 by 21. A term of learning can provide a rollercoaster of emotions as no sooner has a child grasped that the key to percentages is to find 10% of the number and use that to find the other parts, the topic switches and they find themselves like Sisyphus at the bottom of a mathematical mountain, now having to push their rock to the top again, seemingly infinitely.

The quantity of content each child is expected to learn is another cause for difficulty. In Year 6, children sit SATs, Standard Assessment Tests, in May. They are tested on maths, reading and EGPS; another teacher acronym which stands for English Grammar, Punctuation and Spelling. By March or April, the content of Reading and EGPS is complete and the children are honing their skills and practising. In order to give each element of the Maths curriculum enough time to be absorbed, I would still be teaching new content to students right up to the week before their maths SATs. Despite my best efforts, this high pace does generate a rushed feeling which the children can sense. If the teachers are feeling like they can't fit in everything they need to then you can imagine how the children feel.

Combine the sheer weight of content to absorb with the flexibility of mind required to switch from method to method and it's no surprise that maths tests across a child's school career tend to generate more dread than any other.

But all is not lost. Maths schemes that schools use are engaging, varied and keep each topic fresh. Teaching quality, in my experience, is of a very high standard as lots of professional development time is focused on improving the quality of maths teaching in schools. As ever, I believe you can rely on your child's school to be doing the best they can, all we need are a few maths specific tweaks to neutralise the problems mentioned.

In order to meet the challenge of specificity (having to know lots of distinct skills for different topics) we need to focus on the fundamentals that underpin most questions and topics. There is little point in spending a month learning how to order decimal numbers from smallest to largest if it is unlikely to come up in many questions and, more importantly, help in the "real world" when your child leaves school.

The fundamentals:

- Times Tables
- Mental maths
- Reading the question

Let's look at these in more detail.

Times Tables

Times change, but times tables don't. This is something we all remember from our early maths lessons and being able to quickly recall any multiplication up to 12 x 12 will give you and your child the biggest advantage for the least amount of effort. It sounds deceptively simple but almost every topic in maths will rely on knowing times tables, and ideally the way to divide them too. This skill will help your child in: straightforward multiplication, fractions, decimals, percentages, long division, statistics and more complex word problems. That covers around two thirds of the curriculum and increased speed of calculation will give your child more thinking time for the truly tricky topics and questions they come across.

There is no "trick" to learning times tables, and that's a good thing. Rote learning, or learning by remembering and not by deep thought, does seem to be frowned upon in the modern educational landscape, but it has its place. Start with the 2x, 5x and 10x tables, add the 3x, 4x, 6x and finish on the 7x 8x and 9x. 11x is straightforward and 12x can come a little later but will be helpful towards the end of primary.

You can create flashcards or use one of the many "fun" internet-based games to learn each multiplication fact.

I have used data from one internet-based Times Tables game to show the children how beneficial it is. Each child would have a school login to the service and a personal account. They could practice as much or as little as they liked and each week I would review the results. I found, unsurprisingly, that those children with the highest number of correct Times Table answers scored mostly highly on their arithmetic papers in class. More interestingly, however, was that those children who spent the most time (and therefore effort) practicing showed the greatest improvement in their scores from their own starting point. They were simply exposed to the multiplication facts more than their peers and absorbed them. Regardless of how quickly or slowly their accuracy improved, it always did.

Mental Maths

"Why do we have to learn this, Miss? We have calculators!" came the brave challenge from one of my classmates in a freezing cold Year 6 classroom in 1997. This protest was in response to what seemed to be our tenth "Mental Maths" test that week.

The response shot my friend down in flames, "Well, you won't have a calculator in your pocket when you grow up."

Whilst it would be unfair of me to expect my teacher to be able to predict the inception of the smartphone that destroyed the validity of her retort, the skill of being to calculate in one's head remains a stubbornly important part of any child's learning.

Mental calculations don't just help us to estimate the total of our rapidly-inflating shopping bill or how many packs of drinks and crisps are required to placate the children at a party; they help to build our Working Memory.

If you are technically minded, you can imagine Working Memory as the RAM of a computer: the ability to hold information in the short-term to solve a bigger problem. When you have enough, everything runs smoothly and you don't notice it, yet when Working Memory is limited, even relatively simple calculations grind to a halt:

3 Jack buys milk and orange juice from a shop.

£1.45   £2.40

He pays with a £5 note.

How much **change** does Jack get?

This question is lifted from the 2024 SATs that Year 6 test.

When attempting this question yourself, consider how much information you need to hold in your mind, or working memory, at each step.

Step one: Remember that I'm adding these items.

Step two: Hold the £1 + £2 in my head as I calculate 45p add 40p.

Step three: Total cost of the two products is £3.85.

Step four: Keep that price in my head as I pivot to subtract that number away from my £5.00

Step five: Take the £3 from the £5 first and hold that remaining £2 in my working memory as I calculate what would be left after subtracting the remaining £0.85.

Step six: Final amount £1.15

Your working memory was spinning mental plates at each stage to hold your intermediate answers and allow you to move to the next step. For a child with an undeveloped Working Memory, they will likely lose track of where they are and quite possibly being adding when they should subtract or any number of procedural errors.

Mental maths practice allows us to build Working Memory and improve our ability to hold each step in our mind as we progress through more difficult problems.

One useful strategy can be to attempt arithmetic papers without the use of note paper and see how accurate the answers are. You and your child will begin to notice where the slip-ups have occurred and each attempted question is another step toward developing a Working Memory that can store more information in the short term.

A hugely overlooked aspect of using Working Memory is fatigue. It is quite literally tiring to repeatedly hold specific information in your mind, recall it, write it and then repeat this process multiple times under time pressure.

In a Year 6 class of mine, I taught a girl I'll call Ettie. Ettie tried hard with all her learning but really felt the pressure of timed questions. It didn't help that her best friends had no problems with their working memories and would fly through most timed tests without a flicker of concern. Given time, Ettie could answer anything the curriculum could throw at her. I noticed that at the start of a test or lesson, she would cope quite well; keeping up with all that was expected of her. As the day or test progressed, however, she looked visibly tired and frazzled by the constant demands of her working memory. She would often get tearful in lessons and proclaim "I can't do any of it!" before needing a break to recharge.

Ettie didn't need help with the procedure of answering questions. In fact, to spend time repeating a method to her would have just frustrated her quick (and competitive!) mind.

Instead, I took a different approach.

Firstly, Ettie needed to feel less pressure from around her. I orchestrated a whole class move so that she was away from her super-quick mathematician friends. It was counter-productive for her to feel like she was racing others and this had an immediate positive impact on her state of mind.

Secondly, I took time pressure out of the equation. For a while, I asked her to focus on completing as many questions as she could, without targeting reaching the end of a piece of learning or the current test. We would focus on accuracy first and speed later. This gave her the mental breathing room to take each question a step at a time and not become overstimulated and burned out by rushing everything.

The result was that she calmed down and made fewer mistakes. This created a positive feedback loop where she grew in confidence by seeing for herself that she did indeed know the methods. I removed the guard rails over time and gently began to expect her to answer one more question on each test. Knowing she had a competitive side, this seemed to become an enjoyable challenge for her. By stripping away all expectation at the start and building it back in slowly, Ettie returned to almost her original breakneck pace, but now equipped with an improved working memory and less stress. Sometimes we all have to go backward more than we'd like in order to move forward.

Reading the question

There's a reason I wrote about the importance of reading and learning how to comprehend a text at the start of this section. You'd be wrong to think that being a good reader has no place in a maths test and I'd argue it challenges comprehension skills just as much as any "reading" test does.

"What is the question asking you to do?"

Considering this at the start of each new maths challenge would neutralise more errors than any other step a child can take.

Across the span of a week or term, one topic will be taught until it is fully covered. The concept of a "percentage" will be introduced, the teacher will model the method of how to calculate a percentage, the children will try some simple questions and move on to more complex ones when they are comfortable. So far, so good. In the next few lessons, the percentages to calculate will become more complex, from finding 50% to finding 31%, for example. With the basics of the method fresh in their minds, most children manage to keep up with this increasing challenge; their minds are in "Percentages Mode" and, with support, almost all will make progress from their starting point.

So why does it so frequently fall apart when children are challenged with tests? Some teachers and parents seem to believe that their children just haven't retained the knowledge or understood the concept to a deep enough level. Having watched those same children answer questions accurately during a typical week of lessons and then crumble in the face of a test, I don't believe the problem comes from a lack of understanding, more a lack of mental agility when tested on so many things at once.

Simply put, it is difficult to switch from topic to topic in every question. With maths learning requiring an understanding of so many varied skills, it is a huge challenge for a child to answer a question about Long Multiplication, for example, and then quickly adjust to the next question which asks them to calculate the percentage of a number.

In a test scenario, children don't have the benefit of a refresher of the method from their teacher. The "OK, so yesterday we were learning percentages. Remember, the key is to find 10% of the number first and then use that to find the other percentages you need." As they turn the page in a test, a jumbled ball of lesson fragments fly around their head; little memories of a question they were stuck on, trying desperately to recall the way it was shown to them on the board or the key piece of learning that will help them with the problem in front of them.

What the children need isn't more hours of learning, but a quick way to switch "modes" in their head, recall the key to each method and get moving.

"Find 10%"

That was what was written in the Percentages section of my maths display board. Not a fully-worked method or a list of questions, just those seven characters.

I know the class know how to calculate, so I just want them to remember a short punchy phrase that will help them to switch in to "Percentages Mode" and get started.

If I want to find 25% of 200, I first find 10% by dividing by 10 (20) and use that answer to find 5% (half of my 10% figure: 10) and then add them up:

10% = 20
10% = 20
5% = 10
20 + 20 + 10 = 50.

The next question is about adding Fractions. The key phrase?

"Make the denominators the same"

You can't add 1/3 to 1/6 as the size of the denominator, or piece, are different in each. So, convert 1/3 to 2/6 and then they can be added together.

1/3 = 2/6
1/6 + 2/6 = 3/6 or ½.

Next is a huge addition sum.

"Check the symbol."

By reviewing our tests together, we noticed as a class that more children made a mistake because they subtracted when they should have added (or vice versa) than made a calculation error. The key phrase helped them to make sure they were reading the question properly. Many children drew a ring around the "+" to ensure they knew what they were doing.

You can generate the key phrases yourself and asking your child to think of one can be hugely helpful, as they have to summarise a topic down to one sentence which will test their understanding. Failing that, choose a key phrase related to a common error for them.

Phrases like "Kilo means 1000." Or "Percent means per hundred." can be really useful for this.

Once these phrases are in place, the answers will begin to flow. You will likely see a speed and accuracy increase, all without taxing that precious Working Memory. The learning is in there but unless we are able to quickly unlock it, confusion takes over and mistakes are made. Read the question, recall a short key phrase and get moving.

Make notes

Building Working Memory will always pay dividends but it takes time. It's a bit like balancing a household budget; it takes a while to build income but the opportunities to spend less are always there. The best way to make those savings and tax the Working Memory less is to make use of notes.

The objective here is to store that fleeting wisp of information somewhere else than in your head. Even the most skilled mathematicians have a very small window to keep and use this data that's in their head. Psychologists Ricker and Cowan (2010) found that memory of the orientation or colour of simple shapes begins to degrade in just 4 seconds if not refreshed.

Let's remember that we are aiming to support young children who are learning skills for the first time, often under the time pressure of a fast lesson or test. We can therefore safely assume that that duration will be vastly reduced in children and more errors will be made in recall when we have the added pressure of working with a concept we don't yet fully understand.

My advice is to build the habit of teaching our children to take that key information and note it down, freeing up their Working Memory and seemingly relieving the mental pressure and fatigue of holding it in their minds.

Consider this simple example from the 2023 maths SATs test for Year 6:

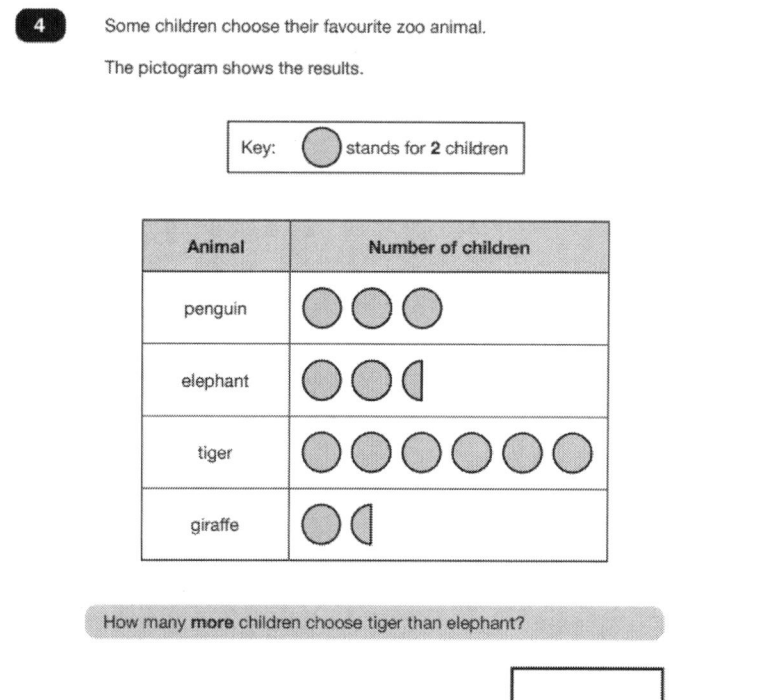

4 Some children choose their favourite zoo animal.

The pictogram shows the results.

Key: ⬤ stands for **2** children

Animal	Number of children
penguin	⬤ ⬤ ⬤
elephant	⬤ ⬤ ◗
tiger	⬤ ⬤ ⬤ ⬤ ⬤ ⬤
giraffe	⬤ ◗

How many **more** children choose tiger than elephant?

1 mark

Take a moment to answer the question for yourself. It's a one-marker, early in the test so this isn't meant to require a MENSA membership, but mistakes can (and will) still be made.

5 children chose the elephant and 12 children chose the tiger. The difference between the two is 7. Congratulations if you got that correct, maybe you still have those primary school maths skills after all.

Below is an example of the same question with a full set of notes:

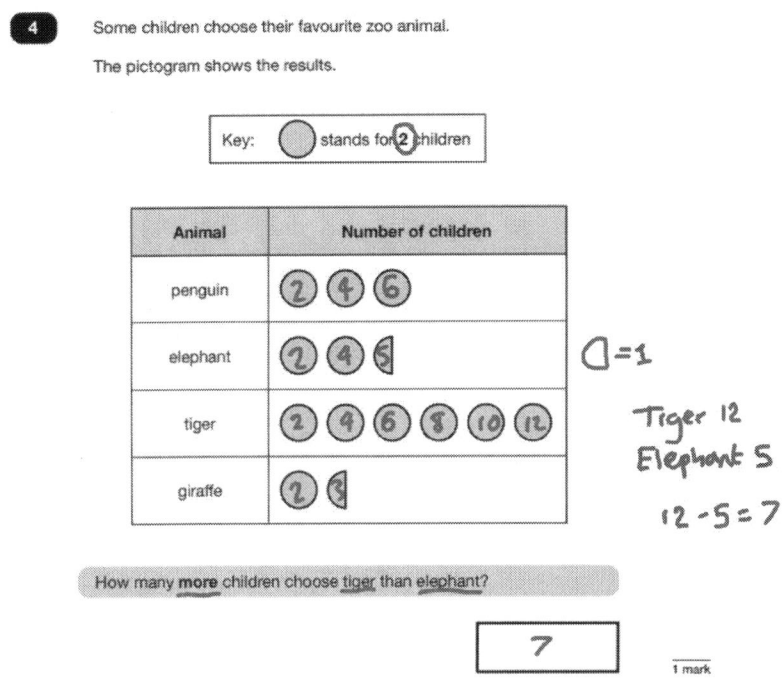

Firstly, I have circled that each full circle equals two children. Those rushing this question will assume one circle = one child. Quickly mark up each column, noting that a half circle must equal one child. Finally look closely at the question to see that we need the figures for just the tiger and the elephant, take one away from the other and you have the answer.

The notes took around 30 seconds to make and are multi-purpose. Firstly, they organise the child and reduce the strain on the working memory by writing down the row totals on the paper so nothing needs to be held in the mind. Secondly, they reduce errors because each phase or section is completed before moving on. Finally, making these notes means that if a child has to return to this question due to lack of time, they have begun to make sense of it and they have a much better chance of getting the mark.

I can predict what you might be thinking. "Why calculate all the rows if the question only mentions the tiger and elephant?"

I teach all my students to make sense of what is in front of them before they even look at the question at the end. We see it's a Pictogram question, recall the key phrase "How much is each symbol worth?" and then get to work on making sense of *all* the data. Many questions will have multiple parts and it is confidence-building to feel that you understand all the information before reading the question and completing the final simple calculation to get the mark.

You might believe, as many of the children do initially, that making these notes would take up valuable test time. As I mentioned, those notes took around 30 seconds to complete and the whole question was wrapped up in around 40 seconds. In this particular test, the children have 40 minutes to try to gain 35 marks. The pacing matches what is needed to answer all questions within the time limit.

More importantly, we can leave this question having confidence that it is correct. There is nothing more demoralising than to rush through a test, getting to the end with time to spare and either getting questions wrong for no reason, or having to backtrack through much trickier questions than the example and having no idea where to start because you have the same blank question that scared you in to flipping the page over in the first place.

To borrow an old military phrase, "Slow is smooth and smooth is fast."

In keeping with our overall goal of simplicity, note-taking needs to be easy to do.

1. Consider which "mode" you need to be in. "Percentages Mode" "Pictogram Mode" etc.
2. Note down the key phrase for that topic or at least recall it. "Find 10%" "What is one symbol worth?"
3. Make short notes to understand what is in front of you, such as those in the example.
4. THEN look at the question and use what you have to find your answer.

In summary, supporting maths learning should be focused around simplifying the learning process. Don't spend more time revising; focus on Times Tables and topics that will be useful in many lessons. Don't try to be fast; take time to read what the question is asking. Don't try to hold all the complicated figures and ideas in your mind; make simple notes to unburden the Working Memory. I always found subtracting easier than adding anyway.

Chapter summary:

- Learning Times Tables and how to calculate mentally will provide the greatest improvements in maths learning for the least amount of effort.

- Create a one sentence key phrase for each topic. Punchy and memorable or your child's working memory will get overloaded.

- Learning to read the question won't score marks on it own, but it saves a lot of lost marks, and that is almost as good.

I

PART III

THE "EXTRAS" – SPECIAL EDUCATIONAL NEEDS, BEING "MORE ABLE", HOMEWORK AND SCREEN TIME

I

SPECIAL EDUCATIONAL NEEDS

Special Educational Needs (SEN) is such an important and emotive topic in the world of teaching. The Department of Education's 2023/24 school census shows that 17.1% of children in state-funded primary schools have SEN status; that's about five children in each class of 30. Chances are you have personal experience in raising a child with SEN or know someone who does. At the introduction of the 2015 SEN Code of Practice; the bible of how to manage SEN in schools, the percentage of SEN students was 14.4% and that number has increased each year since its publication.

Having Special Educational Needs simply means that a child requires extra classroom support due to a disability or learning difficulty. What that extra support looks like at a classroom level can and should look different for each child.

There are four main SEN areas and it is important to discuss these in order to raise awareness and to be able to consider how to effectively support children within each:

1. **Communication and Interaction**
   This includes Autism, Asperger's syndrome, speech difficulties and children that find it challenging to express themselves.

2. **Cognition and Learning**
   This is for children who struggle to keep pace with the learning, even with effective teaching. Specific difficulties could be dyslexia, dyscalculia and dyspraxia.

3. **Social, Emotional and Mental Health**
   A rapidly growing area of need. This includes anxiety, depression, self-harm and ADHD and broadly covers children who need extra support in managing behaviour or relationships at school.

4. **Sensory or physical needs**
   This group is for children with disabilities such as hearing or sight impairments or anything which causes a barrier to learning as the result of a disability.

It is rare for a child to start primary school being categorised as SEN. To say nothing of the difficulties in getting a diagnosis, children are changing and developing so rapidly at age four that what might seem like a critical issue can just as easily be a developmental phase and disappear without much intervention.

UK teachers do not come equipped with any qualification which enables them to diagnose a learning difficulty or disability. They do, however, find themselves in the often tricky situation where they are the first to suggest to a child's parents that believe they need extra support or an emerging need at school. I'm surprised this doesn't cause more conflict that it does as it is rather like being told by your personal trainer that you might have a heart condition; they may well be right but they aren't strictly qualified and, depending on your outlook, you may well take offence at the suggestion.

Fortunately, the vast majority of parents want what is best for their children and obviously value the input from someone who spends so much time with their child.

I have experience teaching children with Autism, ADHD, self-harm issues, severe anxiety, physical disabilities, extremely challenging behaviour and everything in between. I can never be sure of exactly what is wrong but I know what needs to be investigated further or discussed with parents.

Those discussions with parents have to be entered into tactfully, yet they can represent the beginning and end of a SEN investigation.

Whilst providing SEN support to a child does not strictly require the permission or consent of the parents, the SEN Code of Practice states that schools should ensure "decisions are informed by the insights of parents....and young people themselves." Every decision made and the details of the SEN support must be communicated to parents at every stage.

Typically, there is no conflict between the school/teacher's view about a child's SEN status and the parents. Both want the best for the children in their care and are open-minded about how to support emerging needs. However, there are occasions when the expectations of the two groups don't meet neatly in the middle.

Liam, a boy in my Year 6 class, had all the hallmarks of Attention Deficit Hyperactivity Disorder (ADHD): he struggled to focus for more than a few moments on any activity, seemed compelled to want to distract others, would interrupt conversations, blurt out answers during lessons and regularly get in to trouble for impulsive actions in the classroom and in the playground. You might argue that this sounds like many eleven-year-olds you know, but there are subtle nuances to behaviour like Liam's which get teachers to consider a SEN issue rather than a typical behaviour problem. My feeling was that Liam really wanted to be a good student and focus in class but he acted on impulse and couldn't seem to control this.

I had known of Liam when he was a younger student. He would often knock on my classroom door during lunchtimes and ask if there was anything he could help with. He had a boundless energy beyond the realms of a typical primary-age child and he clearly wanted to put it to good use. When he got in to trouble, I saw genuine remorse and he would often berate himself for not thinking before he acted. Special Educational Needs can rarely be defined via a checklist of behaviours; it is the overall picture of a child that guides teachers toward considering getting extra support and adding the child to the SEN register. To me, Liam needed more support than usual so I called in his parents to discuss my thoughts.

I told Liam's mum and dad how he presented in school and I said I would like to add him to the SEN register so we could support him better through tests and in to secondary school. Children on the SEN register are afforded allowances based on their need in SATs tests, whether that be sitting in a quieter room, extra time to finish or someone to read questions. When progressing to secondary school, findings from primary level will be shared with the child's Head of Year or the staff member in charge of transition. This can help the child as the secondary school are aware of behaviours and they can more quickly be supported when they reach the towering buildings (and children!) of "Big School".

However, Liam's parents didn't agree. They believed that other children in the class were distracting Liam and in the times he had been in trouble it was all a misunderstanding. They didn't support the idea of adding him to the SEN register and did not want to progress to the next step on the SEN journey which is to ask a qualified

Educational Psychologist to come to school and observe Liam's behaviour and make a formal diagnosis if necessary.

Unless there is a worrying need to raise SEN concerns, such in cases where a child is being violent to others or having extreme outbursts in school, for example, the school typically honour the parents wishes, as we did in the case of Liam. As Liam's teacher, my opinion is exactly that, just an opinion. Liam continued in my class and was not added to the SEN register. He performed relatively well yet continued to have difficulties with others in the class and his focus. We will never know whether an educational psychologist would have felt it necessary to diagnose Liam with ADHD or whether Liam's parents maybe felt there was some stigma related to having their son on the SEN register, but I feel it is something to investigate until guided otherwise. There would be no cost to anyone and, if diagnosed, Liam would have received more learning support and a greater tolerance for behaviour issues right through to the completion of his compulsory education.

The first key step, then, if you feel your child needs support beyond what a class teacher can provide, is to open a dialogue with them. You don't need a PhD in Psychology or any suggestion of a diagnosis; just an open mind and some good examples of how your son or daughter acts at home. This will add very useful information to the overall picture and help the school determine whether the issues are school-based, home-based or consistent.

Ask the class teacher for a meeting after school and see if the Special Educational Needs Co-ordinator (SENCO) can attend. They will guide you through the process and at very least you will gain an insight in to how your child is progressing at school. The teacher will benefit too. I have lost count of the number of times I have called parents after noticing a child seeming more upset or distracted than usual, only to have a parent explain that there had been a death in the family, a divorce or change of family circumstances, signing off with, "Oh I didn't want to waste your time and call in."

If it affects your children, SEN or not, your class teacher will want to know. We can make subtle adjustments and generally make sure they have a little breathing room to allow their world to stop spinning out of control. It doesn't need to be a face-to-face meeting or even a phone call. After learning about a difficult situation at home for a girl in my class, I phoned her mother and had a quick chat about how I could support her daughter. Following this, I would get a weekly update noted down on a scrap of paper delivered by her daughter as she came to class. Her parents were busy people and they found a way to get information to me without disrupting either of our schedules. Whilst maybe not known for our flexibility, teachers can adapt!

Whilst SEN is, quite rightly, a topic taken seriously by teachers, parents and school management it is crucial to remember that we are all basing our support decisions around how a child copes within a school environment. That may seem obvious on the face of it but if I was running a school based in an outdoor activity centre or an establishment offering sports scholarships, children like Liam would thrive instead of being marked as having difficulties.

Every child has their own strengths and weaknesses and they grow up to become us adults who are afforded some level of choice as to where to work and how to best use these skills. A person who enjoys using logic and calculation and prefers not to deal with grey areas and creative interpretation might make a fantastic accountant or software developer. The assertive, confident, bouncy child who can't sit still and always wants to know everyone else's business would make a brilliant Police Officer. We must keep in mind that, in many cases, we are labelling a child as having Special Educational Needs because they need extra support to succeed in a system that their natural tendencies aren't compatible with.

This is the perfect time to mention Tony, the child I mentioned in my "Educational Landscape in the UK" chapter. Tony's low confidence and SEN made school feel like a daily struggle. However, Tony was an extremely gifted self-taught gymnast. The first time I saw Tony front flip off a school bench whilst eating a biscuit, I had to suspend my disbelief and stifle my usual shouty teacher voice at the breaking of school playground rules. This was the spark of inspiration I needed. I immediately enrolled Tony in extra pre-school gymnastics classes, funded by SEN finances. I made sure he led all demonstrations in our PE classes, performed stunts in class assemblies and he would glow at every well-earned round of applause for his latest trick. Tony had found his area of excellence and he finally knew what success feels like. I can only imagine how different Tony's school life might have been if the Department for Education wanted all children to be proficient in gymnastics.

This is not a call to action aimed at revolutionising our education system; a system that is very effective in teaching our children the key knowledge they need and providing interesting experiences which may inspire their career path, rather it is a suggestion to step back and realise that a child may need support due to a lack of compatibility with school life rather than a fault of parenting or irreconcilable internal issue.

A small but noteworthy number of parents do see SEN support or a diagnosis as a personal criticism. The result is they might decide not to agree to extra support or further investigation, as in cases such as Liam's, but it can also result in conflict with the school.

Recently, I was speaking to a parent about her daughter, Lacey. Lacey had recently been diagnosed with Autism and ongoing behaviour issues in class had caused tension at school that had leaked in to the family's home life. Support and a greater tolerance for emotional outbursts at school were put in place but Lacey's grades continued to suffer and the frequent phone calls home from school were beginning to grate. Lacey's parents wanted more leeway for her behaviour and the school couldn't acquiesce to every demand. Over time, the home-school relationship degraded from collaborative to combative, with Lacey's parents seeing every school sanction as excessive and the school becoming increasingly reluctant to give allowances for challenging behaviour.

In my experience, these conflicts never result in a better outcome for the children and it is worth considering what our goal is as our child moves through the school years.

The education system won't change quickly enough and schools simply cannot agree to a personalised scheme of expectations for every child. Whilst that might seem a noble objective to aim for, a key life skill is to be able to adapt to the situation you find yourself in. It will be easier and less stressful to try to maintain a good relationship and slightly change your outlook and actions at home than to go to war with the nearest education establishment in the hope of changing an entrenched system.

Here are some examples of how that can look in some real-life examples:

Communication and Interaction – See if you can agree with your teacher that your child can have a "learning break": a 5-to 10-minute window where they can leave the classroom (if only to sit on a desk just outside) where they can continue with their learning or cool off. Your child might have a card or note they can pass to the teacher or TA if this is needed. This has had a profound positive impact for some children in my classes with ASD who need more time and quiet to self-regulate when things get loud or intense.

Cognition and Learning – If the learning is too challenging, can your class teacher let you know which topics are coming up in the next week or two? Do they have a study guide, revision video or a simpler activity that your child could try at home so that they get a rolling start on whichever topic comes next? This has the added benefit of removing the dread of not knowing which tricky maths topic you might face when you get to school.

Social, Emotional and Mental Health – How crucial is homework? I have an upcoming chapter on this but could you negotiate a reduction or removal of homework, on the condition that your child completes their learning to a good standard in school? This can provide a little mental breathing room. Another useful item is a journal. If your child doesn't keep a diary or a journal, could they start one that is kept in school? During quiet reading time, they will have the opportunity to vent some of their feelings and, if they feel it would be helpful, share this journal with the teacher so that they know what's on their mind. Journals, shared with consent, have given many children in my classes a way to start a conversation with me about something that is troubling them; often times a conversation they would never have had the confidence to begin verbally.

Sensory or Physical needs – Usually well supported in schools. Consider alternative tech such as a teacher-worn microphone for those with hearing impairments and advising teachers about which physical activities cause discomfort so they can be avoided or worked around without the child themselves having to have a more awkward conversation when PE starts.

There isn't anything "wrong" with your child

Schools have a defined curriculum to teach and they have to create a framework to deliver the most effective learning to children in a way that works for most of them. Currently, we still all work in a system where that involves sitting still at tables for hours a day, listening to an input from a teacher, answering questions and then doing something else in a similar way.

Clearly, this isn't going to work for everyone but it does the job *well enough*. The power of "We've always done it this way." Is as strong in schools as it is in any long-standing organisation and each generation of teachers and headteachers tend to stick to what they know and what they have seen work *well enough* in their careers. It is simply too risky for a headteacher to break the mould and try to redesign their teaching and learning from the ground up in the hope that it provides a more enjoyable and effective learning environment for all. If they were to get it wrong, the metrics they are graded on (let's be honest, test results) would take a dive and they would likely lose their job. As with any behemoth, like the health service, policing or the Government, change is glacially slow and the penalties for sticking one's head above the parapet are severe.

But striving for the system to work *well enough* is beginning to show some considerable cracks. The expectation that test results continue to rise year-on-year is an impossible dream and there is a growing cohort of parents (and teachers, privately) who can see that test results aren't success, they are just the easiest way to rank the thousands of children who take them each year.

The rapidly growing number of SEN children in education is an indicator that whilst the system is frozen in place, the needs of our community are changing. There is increasing pushback against a "one size fits all" approach in all areas of life and being different just isn't so "different" anymore.

Remember that if your child has Special Educational Needs, it means they need extra support to be successful in the existing system. Decades ago, this was interpreted to mean that the child had a problem and their chances of fitting in and getting a good job were somewhat limited. Thank goodness we've removed that veil and we can now see that maybe having SEN is more a symptom of an ill-equipped and stubborn education system than a problem with our kids. As Albert Einstein said, "Everybody is a genius. But if you judge a fish by its ability to climb a tree, it will live its whole life believing that it is stupid." Tony is the perfect example of this quote in action.

As a parent, and as your class teacher, it is our job to support our children through the education system we have. Not with a view to achieving the highest test scores possible, but with the maximum amount of self-worth intact in order that they meet the big wide world knowing that their particular set of skills will be hugely useful to an employer and the world at large. If we can achieve that, we will be doing better than *well enough*.

Chapter summary:

- Having Special Educational Needs is not a failing of you or your child. Be open minded with school as they want to help.

- Talk to your child's class teacher early as, whilst support is available, you need to be proactive in securing it.

- Notice what your child enjoys and does well. Chess, Engineering, Art, Sport; all are valid. Immerse them in what they enjoy as this can mitigate the frustration of finding other subjects difficult.

BEING "MORE ABLE"

The word "ability" as used in schools typically relates to a child's "natural" skill in a subject. The debate around the relative importance of someone's natural skill ceiling versus the impact of good teaching is as old as debate itself. "Nature versus Nurture" certainly has wider implications than just school success, but the way the Education system approaches this timeless argument is of crucial importance to our children. If we choose to take a binary approach for the sake of highlighting the point, a strictly "Nature" viewpoint would result in schools sitting back and allowing children's outcomes to fall where they may, assuming they could not be influenced by teaching. In this case, teachers would be present only to administer learning and observe the output.

The alternative side of the coin would be to assume "Nurture", or in our case teaching quality, accounted for 100% of learning outcomes. Each child, in this case, would be a blank canvas with an equal and theoretically limitless ability to learn as long as the teaching is of the highest possible quality.

As with most binary choices, choosing either one leaves a huge amount of utility unrealised. We all understand that best option is an acknowledgement that children have a varying propensity to learn different skills, yet each can improve if their learning and emotional needs are met.

When I was learning to become a teacher, "ability" was a word we were taught to be very careful around. Describing a child or group as "lower ability" garnered subtle winces from our lecturers and experienced teachers. "We would call that group 'lower attainers' instead." I was told. As an education establishment, we should take the view that children's level of success was a variable we could influence. Describing someone as having a lower or higher ability suggested they were blessed or cursed in some unchangeable way. You'll notice that I didn't say cursed with being lower ability and blessed with being higher ability, as you'll see that the reality is a lot more complicated than it may seem on the surface.

I quickly adapted to removing the word "ability" from my teaching vocabulary and that sat well with my personal values; I believed each child was like a puzzle to be solved and that every person who came to a class of mine, if treated in the correct way, could leave better than they started.

You can imagine my surprise, then, when I was asked near the end of my first academic year in class, to suggest children that might be suitable to join our small cohort of "More Able" children.

Similar to SEN in some ways, this was a teacher-defined list of children who we believed would benefit from extra challenge due to this higher-than-average ability. Any child could be added to this "More Able" group for any subject. Suddenly, ability was a word I could use again and it didn't sit right.

It might not be called "More Able" in your school. Other known labels include: Most Able, Exceptional Learners or Gifted and Talented.

"Gifted and Talented" was the name chosen by the UK government between 2002 and 2010 in an effort to identify children who would benefit from extra tailored support for their "gifts". This programme was scrapped in 2010 and schools were left to choose their elitist group name of choice. Children in these groups are typically offered off-site extra-curricular activities, such as extension maths activities, sports tournaments or writing projects.

In my first year, I had unknowingly inherited some children who were already on the More Able list. Letters were sent home and most of them attended a single event at the end of the academic year, along with groups of similar children from other schools.

I accept that it was and is my responsibility to know who these children were at the beginning of the year but I have to say I'm not sure I would have been able to guess who was on the list before I read it.

Immediately a few concerns came to mind:

Wasn't it attainment, rather than ability, that we were focusing on? I had been operating with the view that any child could improve from their own starting point, yet I now had to select people based on innate skill. The More Able list wasn't known to the whole class, so it felt a little like a secret society and made me feel like somewhere deep in the genetics of the education system, we still believed that some children are just born more capable in some ways than others. It reminded be of the book *Outliers* by Malcolm Gladwell. Young hockey players were highlighted at a young age for what seemed to be their natural ability, scouted and given greater opportunities than other players to develop. They were much more likely to reach the upper echelons of the sport. However, on deeper analysis it was found that the vast majority of these seemingly naturally blessed players were born in January, February or March. As it turns out, it wasn't an astrological quirk; with the cut-off for each hockey Year

Group being the end of the calendar year, the children born in these months were the oldest available to be selected. They were bigger, stronger and more developed in every way compared to those born later in the year. The extra coaching focus was giving these older children the advantage, not some God-given gift.

There isn't a national list of More Able children presented with their month of birth, but with the academic year in the UK starting in September, I wonder and suspect that many of these children might well be the eldest of their Year Groups, benefitting from just having more time alive for their brains to develop when compared to their Summer-born classmates.

In my experience, children are added to the More Able list in the early years of primary school and very few are removed, regardless of academic performance. After all, "ability" is considered to be a fixed attribute: you wouldn't say that Cristiano Ronaldo's footballing ability was gone if he had a bad season. In the same way, once children were on the list, they tended to stay there. That gave rise to my next concern:

"What effect does the "More Able" label have on children's view of themselves?"

Carol Dweck's book, "Mindset" coined the terms "Fixed Mindset" and "Growth Mindset". A fixed mindset is the belief that we are unchanging, have or don't have certain abilities and our skills can't be changed. A growth mindset is the belief that we can change, develop and build our skills based on what happens to us and our response to these events.

We can't categorise ourselves in to one or other of these boxes, and we float between the two quite regularly. If you've ever gotten a bad test result or made a mistake and said to yourself "I'm so stupid!" then that is an expression of a fixed mindset.

"I can't do this."

"I'm just not good at ____"

"I'm not wired up to ____"

"I've never been good at ____"

These are all examples of a fixed mindset. Notice the rigidity. I am a certain way and it can't change.

A growth mindset welcomes in and acknowledges our ability to change.

"I'm not good at this yet."

"I'll get better with a bit of practice."

"I can learn that."

When taught in my classes, I am always so interested to hear how deeply embedded a fixed mindset can be. Yearly, when I explain what a growth mindset is and how shifting our thoughts about ourselves could really help in so many ways, I always hear a variation of this comment:

"I do want a growth mindset but I just can't learn how to do it! I always think this way."

We all have fixed mindset thoughts, the aim is to begin to notice them and to change our language. But fixed mindset thoughts aren't always negative. "I've always been great at maths." Is still a fixed mindset belief and its fragility is only noticed when something goes awry.

For many of the More Able children in my class, the label came with an unspoken pressure. There's no room for a bad day if you believe you are naturally gifted. What happens when you get a bad test result or just don't understand how to measure angles or solve equations? Have you lost your powers overnight? These fixed labels don't allow breathing room to accept that we all have bad days and, when attached to young children with developing brains, they can create a feeling of desperation to live up to a needlessly high and unnecessary expectation.

Cristiano Ronaldo has the life experience to know that a bad match, month or season doesn't mean he has lost the ability to play football. When you're six years old, that isn't so easy.

In my opinion, the whole scheme should be scrapped and teachers and parents should instead focus on embracing failure when it happens and developing a growth mindset in our children that allows them to fail as part of the learning process. A quote on my classroom wall from Michael Jordan says it best:

'I've missed more than 9,000 shots in my career. I've lost almost 300 games. Twenty-six times I've been trusted to take the game-winning shot and missed. I've failed over and over and over again in my life. And that is why I succeed.'

Growth mindset at its best.

However, I'm not here to revolutionise the education system and we have to operate within the culture that we have, whilst hoping for change. So, what can you do as a parent if your child is, or aspires to be, on a More Able list at school?

1. **Support their passions but don't make "More Able" the goal.**

Instil and reinforce a Growth Mindset wherever possible. Explain to your children that effort is more important than attainment and the people we see as "gifted" in some way are usually those that have worked harder than everyone and have just failed and learned more than others. I couldn't offer an example of a successful person who has just been born talented and hasn't had to work to succeed. If this effort feels easy to them then encourage it.

2. **If your child is considered "More Able" then this is the beginning, not the end.**
    Becoming bestowed with the title of being More Able, Gifted and Talented or whichever other name your school uses does not represent the end of the journey where your child gets to bask in the glory of being a complete master at the top of their field. You should consider it more an acknowledgement of potential than a success in itself. They will likely be learning and mixing with other children who are also excellent in their subject.

I remember sending a small group of our More Able students to a regional maths competition. The children chosen from our school completed all school maths learning at a canter. At this regional competition, however, they too were devoured by stronger mathematicians at other schools. Our children had levelled up and were now competing with a different calibre of students. When they returned to class, I could see that they all were surprised and some were downhearted at realising just how competent other children were in our local area. The demoralised decided that they weren't as good at maths as they first thought (Fixed Mindset beliefs) yet for some they felt motivated to focus even harder on their studies so they could compete next year. This is a clear example of the power of a Growth Mindset. These children realised that as they improved, so did their competition and this would always be the case. Meeting this enhanced competition with grace and the desire to be better is the true marker of future success.

3. **Your child might not have found their specialism...yet.**

   As we discussed at the start of the book, the education system is built around measurable metrics primarily based around maths, English and reading. Fantastic if your child enjoys these subjects but this means they will get limited exposure to subjects that they might be fantastic at. Foreign languages, Art, Computing and PE have to take somewhat of a back seat as schools strive to maximise their results in the areas they are graded on. I always wonder how many dormant savants we miss in school purely because they haven't had a chance to experience new activities and therefore never notice how capable they are. As parents and teachers, it is our job to give children an opportunity to have a go at *everything* because who knows what will light a spark or reveal a lifelong passion?

   Let them try a dance class, a free Football session or an after-school Art club. If it lasts a term and they never want to do it again then that's fine, but it all represents good experience for them; both in terms of having the bravery to try new things, getting used to initial failure and building that all important Growth Mindset.

4. **Model the behaviour you want to see.**

   As we grow older, our embedded patterns of behaviour become more entrenched and somehow more difficult to see in ourselves. If you're reluctant to take your son or daughter to a new club, consider that is could be your own Fixed Mindset or limiting beliefs that are bubbling up to the surface. Having been in Chess Club in Year 4 and considered relatively competent, I stopped playing for decades before deciding to pick the game back up a few years ago. Realising how hard I found it to knock the rust off, I found myself thinking "I'm meant to be good at this!" As I lost yet another online game. I starting shying away from playing and losing, all the while being a strong supporter of a Growth Mindset. This struggle to regain my old form illuminated a shortcoming of mine; I want to learn everything *quickly* and I get very frustrated when it doesn't happen as quickly as I'd like. One of my daughters is exactly the same and finds her swimming lessons frustrating when she can't embed a new stroke within the first 30 minutes of learning it. Now she and I are both learning to manage our expectations and try and enjoy the process rather than racing to a finish line that is created by us and only leads to the beginning of a new race.

"But Daddy, you always get mad when you lose a Chess game and you tell me to be patient!" she tells me after a particularly tricky lesson about how to tread water.

It's like being back in Chess Club again; checkmated by a seven-year-old.

Chapter summary:

- Don't aspire to have a "More Able" child. It's not a magic wand for success and many worthy candidates don't get noticed.

- Be aware of the silent added weight of expectation that being "More Able" brings.

- Explore new passions because you never know what hobby or new subject might light a fire in your child.

HOMEWORK

COVID lockdowns were a strange time for all of us in 2020. Every routine we were once used to was dismantled, our ability to travel and even go the shops was suddenly bound by rules around "Social Distancing" and limits around how much we could buy. To add to the challenge of being on national house arrest, most people had to work from home and look after their children, who were also forbidden from heading to class to reduce the spread of disease.

Schools were still open, and I was teaching a much smaller group of "Key Worker children"; the children of people with jobs that were considered critical to the running of the country: paramedics, teachers, police officers, firefighters and more.

Regardless of your appetite for variety, this was an unprecedented period of change and truthfully, nobody knew which way was up. I'm not here to pass comment on the policies that came and went, but I will say that trying to maintain a straight face and Government-approved semi-sombre attitude whilst teaching a group of children in what can only be described as a full-face plastic welding mask, was challenging.

The curriculum as we knew it was put on hold as the Government accepted that most children could not expect to get the same high-quality education at home as they do at school. Yes, that's right, parents were now expected to juggle online meetings for work *and* teach their children at home.

The cracks, predictably, began to show quite quickly. Fortunately, the school I worked at had a functional digital learning platform where short activities could be posted by the teacher, completed at home digitally (either by writing with a stylus to fill in answers or using pictures and video to show their results) and then marked by the teacher when this was all complete.

Very few parents had the time or the skills to support their child's learning whilst also holding down a job. I don't blame them. There is an air of mystery to many about exactly how good teaching is delivered. It can look simple when it goes well, but when you have to suddenly transition from being an Account Manager to a Year 3 teacher, it can be harder than it looks.

Let's remove some of the mystique around the teaching process. In the majority of lessons, it looks like this:

1) The teacher explains what we are learning and demonstrates (or "models") the correct method.
2) The children attempt a simple activity to see if they have absorbed this input and enable the teacher to see where mistakes are being made or if they are confident to continue to more complex ideas
3) A bigger, independent activity is outlined and the children aim to complete this with teacher support.
4) We share what we have learned and build on this in the next lesson.

The huge advantage that teachers have is that they use semi-standardised methods to teach each topic. Thinking back to finding a percentage of a number, I will teach each class to firstly "Find 10%" of a number and use that to find their answer. After teaching 30 children per year for six years, I have also seen everything from instant mastery of this idea, to assuming the answer will always be 10 (because there's a number 10 in the method), to a complete emotional breakdown at the very sight of the question. Therefore, I'm well-equipped to get out ahead of these misconceptions, explain a few when we start and know how to counter the typical errors as they arise.

If you've suddenly had to transition from being a Software Developer to teaching percentages, you now have to conjure up your own method and will likely be blindsided by the multitude of ways that new learners will get things wrong.

Via a series of frantic phone calls with overwhelmed parents I learned that children really don't take well to having the methods they know from school being changed on the fly by their well-meaning but underequipped mum or dad.

School and parents adapted over time, which I was pleased to see. I was becoming increasingly concerned as I noticed that children from disadvantaged backgrounds or those whose parents found school a challenge were submitting less and less learning from home. Arguments were starting and children were refusing or unable to complete what was being asked of them. As worries around COVID faded (or the powers that be realised the system was unsustainable, I'm not sure) all children were back in the classroom, much to the delight of teachers and the families in their care.

Once again, we had returned to the only expectation of home-schooling, a weekly sheet of homework tasks that should take no longer than an hour to complete. But for many, on both sides of the pen and paper, learning at home had become forever tainted and fraught with difficulty.

A dislike of doing yet more learning after school isn't new. Understandably, children have always felt aggrieved about being followed home by school tasks after the day is done.

Typically, the time spent arguing about why homework exists far outweighs the time it would take to actually complete it. As parents we might view this as illogical, but it is a feature of the human condition that almost all of us procrastinate or whine about a task that, when finally completed, was nowhere near as onerous as we imagined it might be. Whether it's phoning the energy company to fix a new deal, emailing the Council to apply for a new garden bin or renewing a Passport, we have all put off tasks we would rather not do. The costs of not completing these adult side-quests can be expensive, messy or even delay a well-earned holiday, yet we rationalise them as something we'll "get around to later", often until a worrying deadline looms. That is worth remembering when your child isn't thrilled about completing more times tables on a Saturday morning.

Thankfully, there are some tried and tested strategies that can improve you and your child's outlook to homework and possibly eradicate the arguments for good.

Homework isn't new learning.

As we all found out during COVID, trying to conjure up new teaching methods at home that will likely conflict with the methods taught in school is a recipe for disaster. Homework, especially at a primary school level, will be focused on consolidating what your child knows and cementing what has been taught in the classroom.

The school day timetable is oversubscribed as it is but there is no expectation that new learning will take place at home. So, take the pressure off yourself. If not all homework is completed, or even if no homework is completed at all, your child will have the opportunity to learn everything they need to in school.

At primary level, try considering homework to be a beneficial option, rather than a necessity. School policy will likely say otherwise, but by removing the idea that there is a pass or fail aspect to homework it can alleviate pressure from everyone in your household. If homework is a source of conflict, choose the most enjoyable activity from the list of tasks and focus on that. If your child likes reading, do a little extra and make note of it. If Spelling is seen as manageable but it is quick and well-tolerated, start there. Find an online times table quiz and spend 10 minutes practising. As with any job we find difficult, it is usually the start that is the hardest part. Once your child has *something* in their homework book, there is a much greater chance of them wanting to build on what they've done and impress their teacher (or you) with their efforts. Start from zero and build up slowly. They won't fall behind if it doesn't all get finished.

Timing

Your children will likely argue that there is never a best time for homework, but there are better and worse options depending on when you and your child feel most alert.

Schools, businesses and most workplaces operate from around 9am to 5pm. Each of us are in some way restricted by this as we have to adapt to our schedule, but we all have a tendency towards peak wakefulness at different times of day; our chronotype.

Most people are broadly aware of chronotypes; most simply broken down into the simple "Morning Lark" or "Night Owl" categories. Your chronotype has a genetic basis and influences when you will naturally choose to go to sleep and wake up if all restrictions are removed. You will likely have a good idea of which of these two camps you belong to already, but studies suggest that whilst 30% of the population are "Morning Larks" and 30% are "Night Owls", the remaining 40% have a neutral chronotype, and don't prefer early mornings or late nights (Roenneberg 2007). Your chronotype is a clear indicator of your body's circadian rhythms; your natural body processes which regulate your sleep-wake cycles.

These days, I wake up at 5am. Thankfully, I sit firmly in the "Morning Lark" category, meaning that that alarm doesn't quite give me the shudder of dread that it probably gives many of you. This isn't to say I *enjoy* waking up at that time, it is just marginally less painful for those who, by their genetics, would rather wake up later.

This habit wasn't primarily initiated due to my burning desire to better myself, or my growth mindset. Rather, it came from the crunching time squeeze of having two little girls and a full-time job.

Modern living has disregarded our chronotype and we all must mould and steel ourselves to be up and ready to be at work at the time our employer decides. Given the genetic basis for our chronotype, we can forgive our children for not wanting to naturally wake up at 6am. I'm yet to see "genetic disposition" listed as a reason for being late to school but I'm sure some enterprising teenager will try it one day.

If each of us has a tendency to feel most awake and sharp at different times of day, this means we should guide our children to complete their homework in this phase. Consider how your son or daughter reacts to being woken up for school. If there is a minimal level of fuss and they seem to wake up quickly, we can assume they are more of a morning person. If, conversely, they seem to be in a comatose state even when they reach school, yet seem to become more energised just as you would like them to be settling down to bed, then they are likely an evening person.

For morning people, try implementing a homework session on a weekend morning or even before school. For the night owls amongst us, consider starting homework after dinner.

A balanced third way which works well for many is to complete some homework straight after school. That way, your child is still in "school mode" and it is neither early nor late which suits the majority of children.

Interestingly, all children's chronotypes shift toward being more of an evening or night person as they reach adolescence. Matthew Walker, in the book "Why We Sleep" explains that teenagers' sleep schedules can shift to be two hours later than when they were younger children. This means that a child who would naturally wake up at 9am could shift to a natural 11am start time. With school – and crucially, exam start times – having unflinching rigidity in the face of this evidence, it can leave all of our children at a considerable wakefulness disadvantage. When they need to be most alert they are hampered by their own genetics to feel drowsy. Despite enthusiastic campaigning from Dr Walker in an effort to adapt school start times, the education system has been characteristically reluctant to change.

At home, however, we can learn to take these changes in to account, consider our teenager's desire to sleep later as a developmental phase rather than laziness, and suggest that the crucial work they do at home be started later in the day. Knowing this information won't eradicate disputes about homework but you're giving you and your child the best chance for peace and high-quality learning.

Pomodor-what?

The Pomodoro technique is beautiful in its simplicity. Each Pomodoro is a 25-minute block of time working, before a short break. If the resistance to homework is that it "takes forever" then negotiate a small amount of time that your child is prepared to work for. For a primary-age child, this might be 10 or 15 minutes. Set a timer and let them do what they can in that Pomodoro block. If they want to stop completely when the timer goes, that's fine.

When tested in my classes, the majority of children tend to want to continue at the end of the block. Again, starting is the hard part and most children don't want to leave an activity unfinished once they've started. 10 minutes is enough to generate momentum and you might be surprised at how keen your child is to carry on once they've gotten pen to paper. Of course, there's an added benefit to giving their homework a flashy Italian name rather than "Multiplication for 25 minutes".

The hands-off approach

In the brightly-coloured and ultra-supportive world of primary school, it is understood that children are learning by making mistakes and there is a comforting amount of tolerance for every error and challenge they face. In the span of a few short years, our children progress from looking and acting like toddlers, to walking home from school on their own and being mean to each other on their newly-acquired mobile phones. Change comes fast and school leaders understand that it's a lot to take in for a young person. This is why missing homework in primary school isn't seen as a major transgression. Secondary school is much different and sanctions for not completing homework or meeting school standards surprise children and their parents combined.

We all have to adapt and secondary school is much more focused on preparing children for their next transition; towards the gleeful world of work. For better or worse, we all need to get used to having to do things we don't want to do, and secondary school staff have a jarringly lower level of tolerance for our children not completing their learning.

Whether that outlook is optimal for our children's development is a debate for another time. As they move in to "Big school" we all need to adapt and accept that homework needs to be completed or there will be some punishment.

In my Year 6 classes, I would make the children aware of this. A little portal into the bigger, greyer and scarier rooms of the local secondary school, if you will. It would go a little like this:

"I am not going to chase you for your homework. (audible gasps from half the class) I'll post it each week and completing it will help you to be the best you can be and really secure your learning. Everything I ask you to do will be linked to what we have learned and I'll try my best to make it interesting. You have two options: learn to build a good habit of completing homework in Year 6, or decide you'll take the easy route now and have to learn the hard way in Year 7 by getting a few homework detentions. You are going to have to learn a lot of new things very quickly in Year 7 and in my opinion, you don't need the pressure of having to build a homework habit in that list."

Of course, I wouldn't dream of delivering a mini-speech like that to a group of Year 1s. But Year 6 can (usually) handle it and this hands-off approach of "you decide" has a strange way of motivating some of the class. Those with a taste for delayed gratification are probably already completing their homework without too much trouble, but shifting the slider away from the carrot and towards the stick can be enough to get some children moving.

The reason I believe this works for many is that independence is what a lot of children crave. Especially at the end of their primary school career, they want to be considered grown-up enough to be in charge of their own decisions and offering a tangible dose of agency hooks in more of the class than you might imagine. The message is "Here's how it's going to be, what you do is up to you." I respect each child enough to make that decision for themselves and if they decide they want to take it easy for the rest of Year 6 then it's nothing a few secondary school lunchtime detentions won't fix. Just don't say I didn't warn you!

As a parent, it's important that you commit to the hands-off approach if you choose to deploy it. If you give your child agency and then complain to their Year 7 head-of-year when they get told off, you undermine yourself and show your child that you'll always jump in when they get in trouble. It's not for everyone but it works for many. Famous Italian educator Maria Montessori said "Never do for a child what they can do for themselves." I could have saved myself a lot of time had I known that pearl of wisdom sooner.

Chapter summary:

- At primary school level, homework won't usually teach your child anything new.

- At secondary school level, new learning via homework is rare and child-driven; they have to go and find out new information but if they aren't enthused then they won't learn much.

- Pick the optimal time of day – morning, straight after school or later evening. Use in-school homework clubs if discipline is an issue.

CLUBS

The main objective of primary school is to teach our children the basic skills needed for life and their careers. Anyone who has seen a 5- or 6-year-old noticing that they can read a short book from cover to cover and feel the empowerment of being able to read road signs on a car journey or product labels in the supermarket can see it is a foundational pillar to them being successful in the wider world. Counting to twenty quickly develops to large multiplication questions that can be completed without a calculator. Learning to form basic letters properly leads to the creation of interesting (and often bizarre) original stories.

Through these curated learning experiences, standardised so that everyone in the class leaves with the same basic skills, preferences quickly become apparent. I've known plenty of children who have asked to stay in at break time to finish a story. Others in Year 6 asking to see some secondary school maths to see if they can tackle what the "big kids" do. And of course, almost everyone wants to score more goals or more points in the new sport they've been shown this term.

Meeting the Government's current criteria for "Age Related Expectations" in reading, writing and maths is a worthy goal, but I think it overlooks an arguably more important aim: unlocking latent skill.

Of course, left to their own devices, most children would opt to be outside playing and would therefore never know if a Degree in Pure Mathematics is within their grasp. As educators, we have selected the key skills that everyone should know and put them in front of every child to see what their potential really is.

One positive aspect of the education system is that with a defined path for each subject spanning primary and secondary school, there is a high ceiling and lots of opportunity to progress as quickly as one might like. Teachers are trained to adapt their teaching to the level that the children are currently at whilst stretching their ability. In a story-writing unit of learning, I might be teaching one child to always remember their full stops and, in the same lesson, be demanding a more complex simile from a child who is looking to become the next J.K Rowling.

Latent skills are those skills that remain dormant until tested or activated. You or I may have the ability within us to become the next World Poker champion or Nuclear Physicist, but if we never pick up a deck of cards or find out what Uranium is, we'll never know. It is the job of a school to offer as many novel experiences as possible to young children so that we can try to trigger these sleeping skills and give every child a chance to find their own version of excellence.

Time, as ever, is limited. With school targets being focused around key skills in maths, reading and writing, schools aren't incentivised to find the next National Hockey superstar or Astronaut. They just want to know what your arithmetic SATs score is.

Universities love to publicise the achievements of their alumni; who became an MP, who played a sport for their country after graduating, who won a Nobel Prize. We assume that because we graduate University as adults, it was the University that shaped us. But University is but a step on the educational path that began at 4 years old. The prize-winning scientist didn't hold their first Bunsen burner at 18 years old; they mixed paint in pre-school and learned that we can use two separate items to create something new. Then they grew a flower in primary school, noting down the variables they changed to generate the tallest plant. They began mixing chemicals in Secondary School and wondered how each element on the Periodic Table was discovered. Only then did they focus on their studies to get the grades to earn a University place. The credentials come later but the passion starts young.

The defined rails of a typical educational journey clearly have the potential to unlock latent skills and cultivate greatness, that is for certain. But to teleport to the upper echelons of any discipline, clubs outside of school time help speed up this process and raise the ceiling of what is possible for our children.

My concern is that the schedules of children are beginning to more closely resemble that of a silicon-valley CEO than a young person who, at their core, just wants to play. High-achievers, or those aspiring to be, are coming to school looking tired and there is undoubtedly a trade-off where focus and performance in the classroom is suffering because the children haven't fully recovered and they are doing too much in their day.

It is challenging to get the balance between school and extra-curricular activities to an optimal level, but we can all agree that key school learning should be preserved ahead of an optional out-of-school pursuit, unless there's a real chance of making a career out of it. Much as many parents would like to believe their child falls in to this category, we have to be realistic and realise that this is highly unlikely.

Clubs should be about growth and joy, not pressure and enduring fatigue. They provide a fantastic way to build skills and teach collaboration. When chosen wisely and monitored closely, clubs complement school learning; when overdone, they stunt progress. Our job as parents is to do our best to find the balance.

Chapter summary:

- In almost all cases, school is more important than a club.

- However, clubs provide opportunities for sporting success that schools cannot match.

- If your child is tired a lot of the time from a club they're part of, consider carefully whether it's worth the physical and emotional effort.

SCREEN TIME

The Internet as a Chocolate Factory

Charlie and the Chocolate Factory is children's book written in 1964 by British author, Roald Dahl. The story follows the journey of five children who win the opportunity to visit the world-famous and highly secretive chocolate factory of Willy Wonka. The children each happen to find a golden ticket in a Wonka chocolate bar and get to journey to a place so new, magical and full of sugar that they cannot believe it is real. It seems like paradise: a world of chocolate rivers, edible flowers and bubblegum that never loses its flavour. However, through a series of bad decisions, not following boundaries and not understanding the mechanics of this new world, four out of the five children have various confectionary-related accidents and only Charlie, the only child whom followed the rules throughout, completes the tour and is given control of the factory.

Children in 1964 would have hoped that a world overflowing with joy and wonder would exist one day. No doubt, they would believe that, given the same opportunities as the five children in the book, they would follow the rules like Charlie did and reap the rewards.

I, and other people born in the late 1980s, are the final generation to have experienced the world both before and after our own modern-day equivalent of Willy Wonka's Chocolate Factory was created: the internet.

Hailed as an unlimited source of the world's information at your fingertips, the internet instantly changed our world when it first became available in homes in the mid-1990s. For the first time we could find out, albeit rather slowly using a dial-up modem, anything we wanted to, without having to use a book.

As internet speeds rapidly increased, the world of the internet blossomed like the edible flowers in the Chocolate Factory. By 2007, the next leap occurred with the invention of the first iPhone. No longer were users tethered to a phone line to gain access to the internet; the "Smartphone" gave everyone a portal to the internet in their pocket, wherever they were.

For anyone born after this time period, I appreciate that I sound like I'm explaining the invention of the horse-drawn carriage or a steam iron. This technology has developed so rapidly and become so ubiquitous globally that even those who were present at its inception struggle to remember a time when it didn't exist and govern our lives in the way it does now.

Today, a person can, and millions do, go to work on the internet, use their phones on the internet for leisure and connect with family and friends digitally more than physically. We all now live in our own version of the Chocolate Factory; surrounded by every kind of pleasure and convenience we could dream of.

In Roald Dahl's book, the first "victim" is Augustus Gloop. Noticing a vast river of flowing chocolate in one of the first rooms, Augustus tastes some and can't stop himself. He continues to drink from the river, unaware of the danger he is in. One slip and he drops in, overcome with greed at being able to finally have an unlimited supply of what he wants.

Many of us, and I fully include myself in this group, act like Augustus when given free access to internet 24/7. I now can't even sit through a set of TV adverts without reaching for my phone and I know I'm not the only one. I grieve the loss of my attention span, and like any addiction, I'm not really sure when I became hooked and only realised when it was too late.

Violet Beauregarde is the next child to lose herself in Willy Wonka's factory. Tempted by an experimental piece of bubblegum, despite being forbidden by Willy Wonka and advised by the other children to leave it alone, Violet eats the gum, swells up and is rolled away and not seen again.

Violet's demise reminds me of the girls and boys I teach each year whom, despite the pleas of e-safety trainers, teachers, parents and well-meaning friends, post pictures and videos of themselves online, thinking that they are in control of the situation. It seems the only way to truly learn that content posted online cannot be "unposted" or effectively deleted is to witness your pictures or controversial words being shared amongst thousands of people in mere minutes.

Violet believed the rules didn't apply to her and that she knew better than the adults and was more worldly-wise. Pre-internet, the mistakes we all made were quickly forgotten about, remembered only through the embellished stories and rumours circulated by others. Today, however, the physical evidence is forever immortalised online and one rogue picture can haunt a young person for a very long time.

Veruca Salt, already burdened by having one of the worst names in history, is next to be punished in the Chocolate Factory. Veruca, used to having her own way, demands ownership of one of the trained squirrels used in the factory to select nuts for the premium chocolate bars. Veruca is used to controlling others and is caught off guard when the squirrels turn on her, label her a "bad nut" and dispose of her down a garbage chute.

To me, Veruca represents the rapidly-changing tides of Social Media sentiment and bullying. In school, children seem to either keep their heads down to avoid bullying, or assertively recruit others to push the spotlight on to someone else. Both are expressions of the low self-confidence inherent in growing through adolescence, but in the world of online social media the phrase "Live by the sword, die by the sword" is worryingly apt. It remains a constant battle to retain "control" of the views of others, and every aggressor is one slip-up away from being turned on, losing their hard-won social status and being abandoned by those who only followed them through fear. I think many young people would choose the garbage chute over that.

Mike Teevee is the final child to suffer in Willy Wonka's world. Obsessed with, you guessed it, television, Mike acts like the stars he sees on his favourite films and is drawn to a pair of TV sets in another experimental room. After seeing an opportunity to be on (or should I say "in") TV himself, Mike jumps inside the equipment and is shrunk and stretched before being retrieved by his family. As he leaves at the end of the book, his father announces that he will be disposing of their own TV as soon as they get home.

Steaming their own videos and becoming a "Youtuber" are the aspirations of many children. They have seen people their age become rich and famous from technology they themselves own. All it would take is the right combination of content and creative skills and they would never need to "work" a day in their lives. Mike's dream, as with young people today, has a more virtuous goal than posting questionable pictures, bullying others or spending hours scrolling on apps, but this too poses problems.

Similar to some of my friends who set their sights on becoming professional footballers, there's no inherent harm in wanting a hobby to become your full-time job. It's only when a young person neglects their qualifications; burning academic bridges that can't easily be rebuilt in the process that causes the concern. As the market for Youtube content becomes more crowded, more extreme content is needed to stand out. Make-up tutorials and live streaming gaming content used to be all it would take to make enough money to retire before you were 20 years old, but this is no longer the case.

If you have never read Charlie and the Chocolate Factory or watched any of the films created to tell the story, you might reasonably believe that Willy Wonka intended to punish the visitors to his workplace. Not so. Like the internet, the Chocolate Factory is neutral towards its guests. Both are fantasy worlds, limitless in their possibilities. Both provide opportunities that most children couldn't even comprehend. And in both, the majority of people think that they understand the unfathomably complex system and that the rules don't apply to them.

Predicting the issues we might face as internet use changes would be as difficult for us today as it would be for people in the 1980s to guess how social media would affect their children. What we can do, however, is use simple strategies to orient ourselves as best we can toward using technology for our benefit and gaining control over the systems we do currently use. That way, as technology shifts, our *thinking* will be changed and we will likely approach it in a healthier way. To put it another way, there's no point in me discussing how to change your privacy settings on a specific named app, because by the time you read this, that app will likely be old news. What we can do is discuss how to approach our app use in general terms, ensuring that advice will be relevant regardless of the tech you use.

Here are some tips to help develop your thinking around screen time that are relevant regardless of the app du jour.

Use app age ratings to your advantage

Almost all social media apps have a minimum age rating of 13 years. This means that the companies who create them do not allow children younger than this to create an account and no personal information is stored by them. There is nothing stopping anyone from lying about their age or stopping parents from opening an account for their child, but the basic age restrictions are clear and almost universal. For parents of primary school age children, then, you have a ready-made reason why your child cannot have Social Media apps.

Knowing this can help when your child says, "But her mum lets her!" Instead of being dragged into a debate, rely on the app's own guidelines. If the company says it's made for children over 13, that's the end of the conversation. This gives you a clear boundary and saves you from being the 'mean parent'.

I should say I don't believe Social Media apps are all bad. In my opinion, their costs (addiction, decreased self-confidence, bullying, wasted time) far outweigh their benefits (connection with others, knowing what others are doing, inspiration via new ideas and content).

Adults now are the first generation of smartphone users. Less than two decades have passed since the first iPhone was released and we don't know the effects they are having on our adult brains, let alone those of our children. But I think we can tell. We know they're grumpier, more easily bored, and harder to reach after time on a screen — and, if we're honest, so are we.

I don't blame them; all those criticisms can be levelled at us adults just as much as our children. But if we can see negative effects then we have a responsibility to change, both our own behaviour and also to prevent our children from becoming immersed in a global technology experiment that we don't know the results of, yet.

Team up

Parents naturally look to others to find out where the "line" is with internet use, clubs, friendship issues and almost everything else. We all feel like we don't know what we're doing and we would love for somebody else to be assertive and help us to make decisions that don't have a binary answer to them. Leverage the contacts you have and decide as a group to set an age for smartphones or social media apps.

I have recently seen a trend towards "No smartphones before 14". Yes, it's an arbitrary age and yes, this group does have a social media page. Irony aside, it is helpful as it defines an age and parents can club together and know that the message they will be giving their children will be standardised across the group.

Don't use screens for emotional regulation

Regardless of the amount of screen time you allow your children, by their assessment it is never enough. Schools are trending toward using digital devices for more and more learning and I believe this is a good thing in terms of giving our children the skills required for the working world. Since leaving University, I can't think of a time where I've had to hand-write anything longer than a page of writing, let alone a story of my own. It would be a reductionist view to then claim that all written work is archaic and doesn't fit in the modern world of Excel spreadsheets and online meetings. The skills of writing will always be important, but we must admit that if most of us use a computer daily then our children will need the skills to use one effectively in their adult life.

Emotional outbursts are a fundamental part of every child's development. Tantrums, for both parents and the child experiencing one, are stressful and all of us would probably rather we find a way to avoid them altogether. For a while, a phone, iPad or tablet seemed to be the magic bullet to stop the spectre of a public meltdown in its tracks. Never before have parents been able to silence a child so quickly when having a meal, an adult conversation or a car journey. I would imagine that most, if not all parents have deployed this strategy at least once. I'm not judging, I've done it many times myself. The problem is never the giving of the device, it's the taking it back that stings.

The adult equivalent is having a drink or a cigarette. When stressed, most of us reach for our own self-regulation tools. As much as we would all like that to be a quiet moment to meditate and sit with whatever overwhelming emotion that is swarming our mind, often we choose a beer to take the edge off, a smoke or a vape as a calming distraction, or maybe a quick scroll on our phones to knock difficult thoughts out of our head. Maybe it's because we as adults have so quickly and silently transitioned to using our phones as a distraction that we see no issue in using it to "help" our children in their moments of frustration.

But just like when we put our phone away or finish your drink, the problem persists. Much as the instant soothing we feel would have us believe our pain is reduced, we know it isn't. And so it is when we take the phone or tablet away from our sons and daughters. You could use any number of countdowns or ultimatums, the frustration always comes back, doesn't it? We are merely sedating the feeling that is there in their head. Nothing gets solved. The magic bullet of technology, like every shortcut ever created when battle-tested, falls short of what we hoped it would achieve.

Sedating or distracting from big feelings isn't just ineffective, it actively stunts the development of coping strategies and emotional self-regulation. If our child's only strategy to settle down anger is to use an app or play a game, they are missing a vital opportunity to learn how to cool themselves down and get centred when things go wrong. Being given a device shifts worryingly quickly from being a useful option to being a critical crutch, leaving our calm questioning and loving support feeling like a flat and colourless second-rate option in comparison.

You should receive no judgement from any parent if you currently use devices to soothe your children. It is only recently that we've had the time to notice the negative effects this strategy has on their young minds. Us adults are only beginning to adapt to prise ourselves away from our phones a little more and I don't blame anyone for trying to find a way to help their child manoeuvre through a fit of rage or sadness. But we have to give it up.

In the short term, it's going to cause more meltdowns. Big ones, probably. It's going to take strength to support and to relearn how to discuss what each of you is feeling and to slowly calm down. It's going to mean your bedtime routine will take longer. It's likely going to cause some car journeys to be much louder and some supermarket trips to be rather embarrassing. But the payoff is worth it. Our children will, through the hard effort of all of us, learn to build their attention span back. Learn to be bored and be OK with this.

Learn that every bout of anger and sadness does eventually pass and it doesn't require a distraction or for any of us to "do" anything to hurry it along.

Resist the temptation to pivot to "educational" apps or games as these are essentially the same thing as games, with a slight reduction in parental guilt built in. If you already parent app-free then I applaud your resilience and forward-thinking attitude. Just keep the "I told you so's" to yourself whilst we all shudder in fear at the idea of the next public mealtime without an iPad.

Chapter summary:

- Adults are using screens too much. So are children.

- The pain of breaking a screen time habit will be worth the improved focus and moods of your children.

- If you aren't sure whether an app is right for your child, sign up yourself! Learn by experience so you are informed.

YOUR CURRICULUM OF KINDNESS

The National Curriculum and The Kindness Curriculum are not mutually exclusive. As I've shown, the challenges of anxiety, friendships, failure, confidence and resilience all have to be addressed at some point; whether we integrate them into a more formalised learning plan or continue to overlook them until the issues become large and loud enough that they cannot be ignored.

We can pretend that our child's worries will fade by themselves or we can sit with them and help them to understand that every emotion is normal. We can say "boys will be boys" when our sons get dumped out of their friendship group, or we can help them to understand that our "friends" shouldn't make us feel worse than being alone. We can continue believing the unhelpful story that failure means you are fundamentally flawed, or we can integrate the truth that nobody learns anything without making errors. We can believe that our child is just one of "The Quiet Ones" or we can show them that their role in school and their community is changeable and they can be more than the person they were when they joined school. And we can evolve beyond hoping that life's knockbacks will naturally build mental toughness and we can begin to look one step ahead of what's coming and be better guides for our children.

This will take effort from all of us. But *it is effort we were putting in anyway.* High-quality teaching will and does tick off the requisite boxes of The National Curriculum, but if we truly want to prepare our children for the wider world, they need high-quality care and that means drawing the elements of the Kindness Curriculum to the surface and not pretending they will work themselves out by default.

I'm not so naïve to believe we can instantly change the education system; it is slow-moving and entrenched in the belief that "we've always done it this way". But we can start at our homes, with our kids and with the next difficult conversation. We can begin by asking the teachers at school how are sons and daughters are in class, not just what grades they are predicted to achieve.

If you take one thing away from this book, let it be this: school is about far more than the lessons. Teachers will naturally strive to refine their delivery and the Government will ensure that the topics children learn will remain relevant to their later lives. It is our job to have faith in that facet of the education system and shift our own towards supporting the emotional development of young people by acknowledging their struggles, reassuring them that challenges are a key part of growing up and guiding them through their journey to maturity.

As I have witnessed on an individual and class basis, the benefits of this new approach are truly transformational and heartening to witness. There is nothing better than seeing a previously anxious young person come to school with the spark back in their eyes, or watching a healthy friendship blossom in the playground. Seeing a "shy" child amaze a class by reading a piece of their writing or amaze themselves with a test result they never thought possible.

Those changes are available to every child and, one day, we will look back and wonder how we ever doubted the power of kindness in education. The small acts, the patient conversations, the courage to care - these are the lessons that last a lifetime.

ACKNOWLEDGEMENTS

Writing a book is much more challenging than I ever let on to my students. It has been good experience of building resilience, over-coming self-doubt and viewing failure as the rocky road to finishing something meaningful. The lessons I hope our children learn early really are challenges we wrestle with throughout our whole lives. Best to start early.

I couldn't have written this book without the support, knowingly or unknowingly, from so many people. I'm grateful to Scarlett, Connie and Immy to being unwaveringly supportive and beautiful inside and out.

To my Mum, thank you for instilling in me the values I hold dear to this day. To my dad, who sadly died during the writing of this book, I hope I made you proud.

To my sisters, Sally and Jennie, for always being there to speak to during difficult times.

To my teaching colleagues, I am grateful to have had the opportunity to work with some of the most caring and hard-working people in this world – despite the fact that us educators famously only work from 9am to 3pm...

A special mention to my mentors: Hannah Leach (now Allen) and Roo Elliot. You two sparked a love of teaching in me that I didn't know I had. Your students are lucky to have you.

As we wrap up The Kindness Curriculum, I know that some of you will want to take a deeper look at some of the concepts mentioned. Here is a short selection of recommended reads that helped support the creation of this book.

Recommended Reading

- Dweck, C. S. (2006) *Mindset: The new psychology of success.* New York: Random House.
- Walker, M. (2017) *Why we sleep: The new science of sleep and dreams.* London: Penguin.
- Gladwell, M. (2008) *Outliers: The story of success.* New York: Little, Brown and Company.
- Montessori, M. (1967) *The discovery of the child.* New York: Ballantine Books.

For those who would like to see the full range of research and references that informed this book, I've included a complete list below.

Further Reading

- Dweck, C. S. (2006) *Mindset: The new psychology of success.* New York: Random House.
- Gladwell, M. (2008) *Outliers: The story of success.* New York: Little, Brown and Company.
- Montaruli, A., Castelli, L., Mulè, A., Scurati, R., Esposito, F. and Roveda, E. (2021) 'Biological rhythm and chronotype: new perspectives in chronobiology', *Frontiers in Psychology,* 12, p. 700. doi:10.3389/fpsyg.2021.700.
- Montessori, M. (1967) *The discovery of the child.* New York: Ballantine Books.
- NHS Greater Glasgow and Clyde (n.d.) *Attention and concentration in children.* Available at: https://www.nhsggc.

org.uk/kids/resources/ot-activityinformation-sheets/attention-and-concentration/ (Accessed: 20 January 2025).

- Ridgway, V. F. (1956) 'Dysfunctional consequences of performance measurements', *Administrative Science Quarterly*, 1(2), pp. 240–247. doi:10.2307/2390989.

- Roenneberg, T. (2007) *Internal time: Chronotypes, social jet lag, and why you're so tired*. Cambridge, MA: Harvard University Press.

- Ricker, T. J., & Cowan, N. (2010). *Loss of visual working memory within seconds: The combined use of refreshable and non-refreshable features. Journal of Experimental Psychology: Learning, Memory, and Cognition*, 36(6), 1355–1368.

- Standards and Testing Agency (2023) *Key stage 2 mathematics: Paper 2 reasoning*. Available at: https://assets.publishing.service.gov.uk/media/646626e00b-72d3001334476e/2023_key_stage_2_mathematics_Paper_2_reasoning.pdf (Accessed: 20 January 2025).

- Vygotsky, L. S. (1978) *Mind in society: The development of higher psychological processes*. Cambridge, MA: Harvard University Press.

- Walker, M. (2017) *Why we sleep: The new science of sleep and dreams*. London: Penguin.

- Waterman, A.H. (2017) 'Do actions speak louder than words? Examining children's performance following observed versus verbally instructed tasks', *Frontiers in Psychology*, 8, p. 1485. doi:10.3389/fpsyg.2017.01485.

The quote "Everybody is a genius. But if you judge a fish by its ability to climb a tree, it will live its whole life believing it is stupid" is popularly attributed to Albert Einstein, but no verifiable source exists.

ABOUT THE AUTHOR

Geoff Biddall is a primary school teacher from England with many years of experience working with children and families. His teaching has always focused on helping children feel confident, resilient, and supported in both their learning and their wellbeing.

As a father, Geoff understands first-hand the challenges parents face in balancing academic success with emotional health. *The Kindness Curriculum* grew from his belief that kindness, patience, and understanding are just as important as test scores and grades.

When he isn't teaching or writing, Geoff enjoys spending time with his wife Scarlett and their daughters Connie and Immy. He also loves storytelling, exploring new ideas for children's books, and the occasional chess match.

You can connect with Geoff on TikTok @kindnesscurriculum2025 or www.thekindnesscurriculum.co.uk

You can email Geoff at geoffbiddall@gmail.com

Printed in Dunstable, United Kingdom

70465124R00087